MENTCHU-HOTEP
— AND THE —
SPIRIT OF THE
MEDJAY

BOOK ONE

MFUNDISHI JHUTYMS KA EN HERU
HASSAN KAMAU SALIM

Cover: Logo and design by Mfundishi Jhutyms Ka en
Heru Hassan Kamau Salim

Inquiries and Book Orders should be addressed to:

Great Writers Media
Email: info@greatwritersmedia.com
Phone: 877-556-0487

ISBN: 979-8-89175-033-3 (sc)
ISBN: 979-8-89175-034-0 (ebook)

Rev 12/21/2020

DEDICATION

To my father who connects me to Afraka and a bloodline of spiritual warriors. To my mother who taught me leadership and responsibility. To my sister and brothers who continue to give me unconditional love, respect, and support. To my children, Zuwena and Hassan Iman Salim, who taught me how to be a loving and supporting parent. To my children's mother, thank you for allowing me to be a cocreator. To my mate Ifasewa who is teaching me good character. To the Shrine of Jhuty Heru Neb-Hu, my spiritual family and all my blood family, thank you for your love, respect, and support. And last but not least, to all my teachers, *Dua Ntchr*! This book is dedicated to all the spiritual warriors, past and present. May this work inspire you to greatness and to complete the great works of our Afrakan ancestors.

FOREWORD BY ROSALIND JEFFRIES, PhD

Mfundishi Jhutyms Hassan Kamau Salim was born of the womb of an African American woman inseminated by a father whose spirit comes from Tanzania, where Mfundishi later traveled and where Mfundishi Jhutyms Hassan Kamau Salim as a bloodline son, was initiated through traditional rituals. Therefore, it is not surprising that one of the chapters is on the theme of initiation. As an author, he is a researcher of antiquities, an ourstorian, a storyteller, a performer, a lecturer, and a *Kemety Hem Sem Tepy* (high priest). Within himself is the consciousness of many places and time periods. His descriptions of places like Upper and Lower Kash, Napata, Abu, Punt, Meroe, Yam, Kilwa, Waset, Iwent, Abedju, Ruwenzori, Indus Valley, Tigrus- Euphrates River, Shang Yellow River, Upper and Lower Nile, Libya, and Sumeria are real in geography. And yet there are Atlantis and Lamuria envisioned by the Greek Plato, but here in this African-centered palette, it seems more than imagination. That newness is being a projection from a greater context of global grids in the sky and beneath the earth. In African-centric thought, the black hole in the sky is not a hole but whole. It is like the Kemety *Hr*, which is described in the hieroglyphic dictionary as upon or the black face of heaven. The language glyph for it is the full-view face of a man from Kash, Nubia, Ethiopia. With the divine Ntchr in the deep spaces above, the far reaches is thought to be mirrored on earth in such like the divine black panther. Rich, plush black velvet whether in the sky or on earth, the author's recanting of the saga is the mystery of transformation itself and is from celestial to terrestrial, superhuman being to divine animal, then human, and back again. The priest-author teaches that true reality is invisible. Our perceptions are illusions. We are light energy beings; thus, the Kemety cosmogram, ontology, and epistemology center the power of the sun and calls it Ra. It centers the power of Amen, black kem of Kemet, as a force likewise capable of producing light.

Mfundishi Jhutyms selects Mentchu-hotep of the so-called eleventh dynasty as the ideal hero, the enthroned force of the Ntchr. He is the divine symbolic black panther like the leopard societies upon a pedestal to rule his people. Since not very much was written about this important royal ruler, extra research was involved to fill in the missing pages. The first part of the name is "warrior superior," and the suffix *hotep* is a Kemety word for "peace." Opposites converge, the action skilled one when in battle to defend is awesome, and he is the same one who incorporates a peace beyond our comprehension. It is the peace that restores order, justice, and balance and is the foundation for urban civilizations along the Nile. These enormous successes in building for eternity were great enough to feed the hungry in surrounding nations. The arts and sciences depicted in this book were introduced into the world because its time had come. The fullness of time had come from a long gestation period of birth, stability, and order. The unification of the collective, communal, and corporative came from the reconciliation of upper and lower lands in predynastic Narmer/Menes. His battle, like that of Mentchu-hotep, was to protect the riches therein. Contemplated divine values had been given from above, had been named, and had been studied—Ma'at, Seshat, Ptah. In fact, Mfundishi uses names of characters in this work, the Mdw Ntchr hieroglyphic translations of these are teaching points: Ka-f-Ptah, Mery-en-Ra, Shemsu Heru Tut- Ankh-Ra, Hmt Nswt Wrt, Nswt Intef-Sa-Ra, Medjay Sia-en-hotep.

The name Medjay is well-defined and comes out of the most ancient of African Mentchu combat arts. It is a hierarchal system of highly disciplined men who, in secret societies, developed their manhood in years for mastery under a special *Jegna* (mental, physical, and spiritual guides that help you on your special mission in life). Mfundishi himself, a grand master in these arts, describes in detailed combinations of movements the average persons are not familiar with. The reason is that Africans combined these so-called magic—*Sia, heka,* nature, sciences, and quantum physics—with high performance. As masters, they could travel solo or by the hundreds. He says they could bend knives and swords with their bodies; catch arrows out of the air; eat fire without being burned; dance on glass without being cut; control body temperature, blood flow, and pulse; and pick up balls of fire with a bare hand. They understood Ntchr in a real and esoteric way that is activated in air, fire, water, earth, and spirit and the domains of plant, mineral, and animal, as well as within themselves. His quote is, "The nature of the self is to understand the nature of the Ntchru."

When I lived in the Ivory Coast in 1966–1967, up the country in the Senufo region noted for the performance art of the danced firespitter helmet sculptures, I saw men eat fire, then spit out a fine yard-long laser beam. In the neighborhood of Abidjan where I lived, I saw a man perform with a drummer, and the performer hammered a long nail into his own face. Then with his face close to mine for my inspection, he pulled the nail out of his face with no blood or any mark present upon his face after. What was previously thought to be fiction was, indeed, in this context based upon some other sense of reality or the absorption of some nature spirit.

Mfundishi describes the Medjay masters of the Mentchu combat arts. So phenomenal were they that they were perceived as supernatural. They were astronomers, knowledgeable like avatars with like birth destinies. In the Christian Bible, at the birth of Jesus Christ, the scriptures tell that wise men came who were called the Magi. The word *Magi* is presumed to be a version of the word *magic*. *Magic* is a derivation from the older Kemety system *Medjay*. The phrase *wise men* covered a list of abilities: teacher, prophet, herbalist, and alchemist knowledgeable in smelting of metals and knowing about gems and stones. Especially, they were sky watchers, keepers of time. Verses say that they followed the star of Bethlehem, believing that an unusual soul would be born from the heavens and into a specific geographical area. The Christ with many names was called the Bright and Morning Star. Frankincense and myrrh were given to him. Mfundishi has studied the crystals, stones, and gems of Kemet and adds these within his texts. Long before Christianity and Jesus being called Prince of Peace, Hotep on the horizon, Kemet in three different golden ages had produced princes of peace. Mentchu-hotep was one of these—a military warrior with *hotep*, "peace," in the name. And after him was Akhenaten. To call the Medjay magicians a Western term is a misrepresentation of the fullness of who they were. Their spiritual gifts were natural in Ntchr and followed an age-old regiment in the sciences.

Biblical scriptures do not number three wise men. It is a popular commercial advertisement that dwarfed the count. It was likely three hundred or more, alluding to an older secret widespread order that was in existence in Kemet, the chosen predecessors on a divine mission. The quintessential Jesus message of resurrection from the dead was an indelible imprint, a prophecy taken from the earlier Kemety theme, which is the resurrection of light, symbol of the divine Ntchr as the sunrise and sunset surviving down into the Amdwat to come back with renewed life. The resurrection of the soul and the spirit, the Ka and Ba, of the deceased coming forth by day and by night is ushered into the judgment hall. That was written into the earliest of Kemet texts and painted into manuscripts, walls of temples, and tombs. Mfundishi is not Christian or Islamic but is interested in the primal sources that existed before these religions came about, and his thinking is based upon symptomatic thought.

The deliberate African-centric tone of this work is a desired balance meant to rectify the falsifications of history from the abuses of the colonial periods and the segregation era of false stereotypes. Negative stereotypes resulted in political and economic exploitation, such that even today, the images of men and women have suffered. Beyond pigmentocracy, this book has a tender regard for women as mothers and also for the beauty and graces so typical of the feminine gender. Woman equality is there, and she too sits upon the throne and learns parallel arts to wield the sword and draw the bow of Ta-Sety. Enthroned (Queen) Hmt Nswt wrt Tiyi ruled over Kemet and also the land beyond the African continent. The black woman in mythology gave birth to all humanity and swallowed and bought forth the sun.

The fact is that many disciplines now all agree on the African origins of us all. There is no longer need for proof since science now speaks as one voice: anthropology, archaeology, genetics, melanin studies, language origins, prehistoric cave art, and walls and ruins—all are in agreement. They all point to Africa as the human origin. These one people called by many names then diffused into all other continents of the globe—the San, Twa, Anu, Mbuti, Khoi Khoi, Kung, Batwa,

Batswana, many names but one person regardless of height. In anthropology is Dr. Richard and Mary Leakey; archaeology, Dr. Donald Johensen; genetics, Dr. Spenser Wells; language origins, Dr. Richard Greenberg; Dr. Gabriel Oyibo, an Igbo Nigerian in physics's unified field theory and of origin beyond Einstein with an affinity with Kemety facts of energy and mathematics; and melanin studies within anthropology, linguistics, cross-cultural origins are the masters Cheikh Anta Diop, Senegalese, and Theophile Obenga from the Kongo, my teachers and that of the author of this book. And to the scholars and the masses to whom we have the book written decades ago, the *Wonderful Ethiopians of the Ancient Cushite Empire: Origins of Civilizations* authored by Drusilla Dunjee Houston.

In the past few years, the works of paleontologist Paul Sereno on the faculty of the University of Chicago and contributor to *National Geographic* went to the lower Sahara in search of dinosaur bones and instead found thousands of bones of humans dating ten thousand years. It was so early that the pyramids on the Giza Plateau of Egypt were not yet built. Mfundishi used some of his illustrations and photographs from *National Geographic,* and this was the same professional magazine that in February 2000, boldly published for the massive public the image of dark Africans with Bantu features as master rulers and warriors. Photographs speak, on the cover was sent our imposing strength from the southern source of Kemet. In an erect posture and arms locked across the chest was a Nswt Medjay with monumental pyramids in the backdrop. The cover captioned the message, "The Black Pharaohs of Nubia."

In similar truthful reporting of science and excavations was the *National Geographic* reporting on Dr. Paul Sereno's reconstruction work of thousands of human bones. Samples were taken to the laboratories of the University of Chicago, and here was reported two types of skeletons of the prehistoric lower Sahara, one of them tall and the other shorter. The skeletons were nearly complete specimens of *Sarcosuchus imperator* known as Super Croc. It was fully human, not ape. The site was the Gadoufaoua and Tenere Deserts of Niger. Their descendants today are more than 160,000 and 200,000 among the tribes in fifteen lineage groups—Gorebo, Kiffian, and Wodaabe. They inhabit Niger, northern Cameroon, Chad, Ghana, and Nigeria. Surrounding them are the Hausa and Tuareg.

Dr. Cheikh Anta Diop has proven that the Fulani, Peul, and others have once resided at the Nile River then migrated. In art history, I have been for years making such cultural comparisons of the art of West, Central, and South Africa linked to the advancements made from the Nile and other areas. The Nok of Nigeria is now redated 2,000 BC says Dr. Fred Lamp of Yale University, my alma mater school. I have lectured about these cultures and the diffusion of them and their flux and reflux to and from Egypt, Nubia, and Ethiopia for many years. My specialty includes the prehistoric cave art showing Kemety affinities, and my writings were published back in 1984 by Dr. Ivan Van Sertima, editor of *Black Women in Antiquity* and the essay "The Image of Women in Prehistoric Cave Art."

Over the years, I have taught multicultural global studies on the college level. The current students to whom I teach visual arts are seeking to become filmmakers, animators, digital photographers, and illustrators. Film scriptwriters with zeal and futuristic intent science fiction and virtual reality often base their scripts upon existing literary classics and also ancient mythology. In the amalgamated mix, global boundary lines are crossed in order to create a corpus of materials useful for inspiration and action movies. Especially now, the vast

Internet is a reservoir of intermingling cultures like never before, and that makes the writings of Mfundishi Jhutyms Hassan Kamau Salim the more important. Mfundishi's aim is to penetrate the truths of ancient Kemet especially reclaiming what could be easily lost in the rewriting of history and culture.

INTRODUCTION

Like our great and victorious spiritual warriors of our glorious Afrakan past, we must reclaim and resurrect the Heru consciousness lying dormant in our black Afrakan minds. We must master past lessons so we can move into the future, wise, courageous, and victorious, and once again be in control of our destiny.

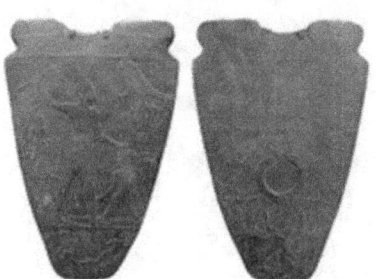 

Reverse and obverse sides of Narmer Palette and bottom center uniter of Upper and Lower Kmt, Narmer along many other great Black Afrakan leaders of the first and second golden ages of ancient Kemet.

From the inception of Shemsu Heru at the end of the fourth millennium BCE, Kemet civilization had gone from strength to strength in every sphere of arts and science and technology, reaching its zenith with Khufu's great monument at Giza. These great and powerful black Afrakan men who came from up south to civilize the Hapy Valley called themselves Shemsu Heru. These Shemsu Heru of Kemet and Kash had become complacent and undefeated in warfare. Superior metal weaponry and nature had placed them within the sheltering and protective desert-backed cliffs of the Hapy Valley. The shock of the breakdown of that essential concept of stability, called Ma'at, at the end of the first golden age of the reunification of Kemet started by Heru Narmer around 4240 BCE or 1 ST (Sema Tawy) was unthinkable. Just like a previous golden age that came to an end as a result of the last great flood, which took place around 12,000 to 10,000 BCE. So from 1 ST until 2059 ST or 2181 BCE, a little over two thousand years of Ma'at and great stability came to an end. Yes, to the Kemetyu, the unimaginable happened. The sacred Hapy floods no longer came or diminished in size greatly for the next 140 years' chaos that reigned or the rule of Set over Heru.

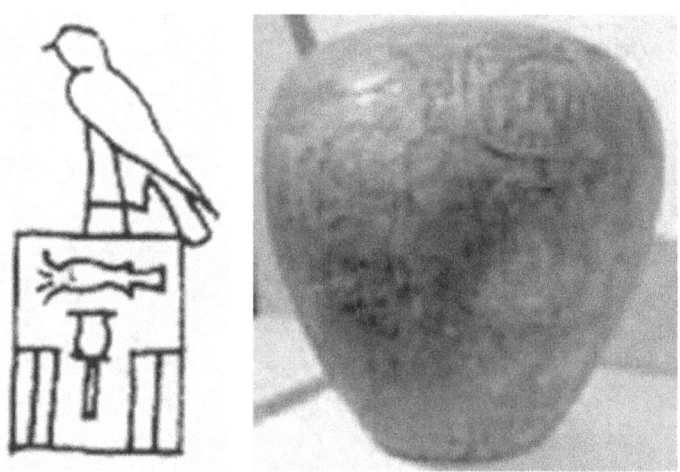

Shemsu Heru Narmer and his mace head

Shortly after the death of Shemsu Heru Nefer-Ka-Ra, Sa Ra Pepy, the central government broke down completely, and the powerful unity that existed between the two lands, Upper and Lower Kemet, fell into disarray. When the Hapy floods failed to fertilize the land, chaos replaced Ma'at while the descendants of Shemsu Heru Nefer-Ka-Ra, Sa Ra Pepy fought over rulership, and as a result, the once powerful nation was divided into many different divisions with none having great power. These weak rulers controlled the area around the city of Ineb Hedj

(Memphis). During this confusion and drought, Asiatics had invaded the delta from the east. The Kemetyu from Waset in the south broke away and controlled Upper Kemet. Following the breakdown of the Memphite government, the provinces began to jockey for power as monarchs set themselves up as petty warlords. It was at this time that a ruling family from Hwt-nen-nesu emerged, founded by Shemsu Heru Mery-ib-Ra, Sa Ra Khety. This Shemsu Heru held power over all of Kemet for about thirty years, but with the help from powerful neighbors from Kash called the Medjay, a dual sovereignty was set up with southern Kemet controlled from a ruling family from Waset and northern Kemet controlled by a ruling family from Hwt-nen-nesu.

After Kemet had been divided once again, two more rulers came to power in northern Kemet's strong families, Shemsu Heru Mery-ka-Ra and Shemsu Heru Ka-nefer-Ra. The fourth and final northern ruler was Shemsu Heru Nswt Bety Khety Neb-kau-Ra of Hwt-nen-nesu, meaning "house of the royal child." He was the ruler who is on the throne during the "Tale of the Articulate Farmer." This story would become a classic folktale that would be taught in all of Kemet for the next two thousand years. Another name for this classic story is "The Eloquent Peasant." This story takes place during the poor Hapy floods and turmoil of the first intermediate period. A poor farmer was robbed of his goods on the way to the market by a local bully landowner. The farmer decided to take the case to Hwt-nen-nesu, the highest court in the land. He pleaded his case in the reign of His Majesty Nswt Bety Neb-kau-Ra, who was entranced by the humble farmer's eloquence. The royal court detained the articulate farmer, and a scribe recorded his arguments, making him present his case time and again in order to enjoy listening to him. Finally, Ma'at prevailed, and the articulate farmer won his case.

As the authority of the northern family of the Hwt-nen-nesu government grew, so did that of the southern family in Waset. Increasing hostility between the two powers resulted in frequent clashes along the border mainly near Abedju (Abydos), which only stopped when Kemet was finally reunited by Nswt Bety Mentchu-hotep.

At the beginning of the second golden age or glorious middle period, sometimes called the classical period of the reunification of ancient Kemet, there were three Shemsu Heru who all carried the name Intef:The Nswt Intef-Sa-Ra Shemsu Heru Sehertawy from 2134 to 2117 BCE or 2171 to 2180 ST died in battle fighting against his northern rivalry kings, but he managed to advance the border of southern Kemet to the city of Iwenet (Dendarah) before he died in battle after ruling for seventeen years. His brother picked up the torch and became the next Shemsu Heru of southern Kemet known as Intef Aa, Sa Ra Shemsu Heru Wah-ankh from 2117 to 2069 BCE. He ruled southern Kemet for forty-eight years, and he was in constant conflict and war against his northern rivalry over the control of all of Kemet. He managed to advance the border of southern Kemet to the city of Abedju (Abydos) in 2228 ST. After his death is Intef Sa Ra, Shemsu Heru Nakht-neb- tep-nefer. He pushed the border yet farther north, almost to Asyut. And this was the frontier that his son, the next Shemsu Heru and the true founder of the second golden age, Nswt Bety Mentchu-hotep fought and was victorious for control of the whole country of Kemet, Sema Tawy (the United Two Lands).

CHAPTER 1

THE JOURNEY INTO KNOWLEDGE

Intef Sa Ra, Shemsu Heru Nakht Neb-Tep-Nefer, the supreme ruler of Upper Kemet sent his son Mentchu-hotep to the great temple of Waset to study under the great warrior and master priest Hem Sem Tepy Dagi of the temple of Amen because one day, Prince Mentchu- hotep was to succeed his father as ruler of southern Kemet. The great warrior-priest was to teach the boy the basics of being a good ruler and a silent, mighty warrior for Ma'at like his father, his father's older brother, his grandfather, and his great-grandfather.

"Mentchu-hotep, my son, listen carefully to what I'm about to say to you. Every soul, every culture, every land has something profound to teach us about what our journey to earth is all about and what the spirit world is trying to say to us. You must learn to make wise choices as a leader. We need to always bear in mind the resources that are ours to use. Always seek the truth, my son. For the seekers of truth, there are no limitations. Where one vision ends, another vision is just beginning. And when we finally grasp one life lesson, another lesson is just beginning. One day you will be like the caterpillar that becomes the butterfly, you will become a Medjay. And

1

when you are a Medjay priest-scientist, you will be one with all creation even while you are in your illusionary body. "Son, nobody can experience our lives for us. I cannot hold your hand through this journey, but I need you to know in spirit, I will always be there because the spirit cannot be destroyed."

He held his nine-year-old son in his arms and kissed him on the forehead, and then the king's hunting dogs jumped all over Mentchu- hotep, licking him all over his face.

When the young crown prince Mentchu-hotep arrived at the great temple of Amen, he was amazed at its beauty and its size. He thought, *What wealth! One day this shall be mine, and I shall make it even more glorious.* His father's palace was large and wealthy, but not like this. At that point, he thought about his lessons on wealth. Wealth's primary function was to enable one to be generous and to bring balance where there was none. The Hem-Ntchr-Tepy (high priest) Dagi escorted him around personally, explaining the special materials, stones and gemstones, and their special qualities, where they were from, and why they were used in the construction of this sacred temple.

"Your father is my mother's brother, so he is my father also. And he is my personal friend, besides being one of the greatest and most just men in all of Kemet. It is an honor for me to be trusted in the enlightenment of your education, your journey into knowledge. You have been truly honored with a great name. It is also the name of your great-grandfather who established our family rule here in Waset. Waset, Napata, Ta-Sety, Meroe, and Yam are all physically, mentally, and spiritually connected, reaching back into ancient times even before the great flood. I know you must have many questions, but they will have to wait until tomorrow. After you have eaten and rested, we will begin your journey. You must study the forty-two books of Jhuty, the Emerald Tablets, the Maxims of Hotep-Ptah, the Mer Khut Pyramid Text of Unas and Pepy, the Eloquent Peasant, and the works of Imhotep just like your father did and your father's brothers and their father's father." He smacked his hands together twice, and two of the most beautiful women I had ever seen came and escorted me to my quarters outside of the palace walls. Both of these women were very shapely but tall and very dark in complexion with a unique kind of makeup that seemed to glitter in the light of Ra. One of the ladies wore her hair in natural braids, and the other had long locks that draped her small shoulders. I was mesmerized by their beauty and rhythm, and I kept bumping into things because I couldn't keep my eyes off them as they danced in front of me. I was to learn later that they were Kashite princesses from Napata, skilled in dance, music, and singing. They were part of a Kemet-Kash exchange program, studying their priestship of Het Heru and Ast here in Kemet at Waset.

* * *

"Mother, why must Mentchu-hotep move out of our palace when it is so large and elegant. Plus, there is no teacher better than you, the Nswt Intef has mentioned this several times."

"Neferu, you will understand one day. At nine years, it is time for a boy to be around his peers so he can grow naturally."

"But he is growing very fast, he is already taller than most of the boys his age and much smarter too, Mother."

"Neferu, only men can teach boys to be men. We as women can give them love, nurture them, and guide them. But if he is to be a warrior-priest like his great and mighty ancestors, we must love him and encourage him from a distance."

"I will try, Mother, but my brother is my best friend. I shall write to him every day."

"Neferu, he is only two temples away." "I don't care, I miss him so much." "He only left yesterday, Neferu."

"*Tiw*, yes, I know, but that seems like Jet, eternity."

* * *

The young prince sat in his new room, contemplating this new shift of events in his young life.

Most of my education up until now had been by private tutors, my parents, and royal relatives. But once I entered the great temple of Ipet Resewt, everything changed. Now my teachers were all priests and divine healers from Kash and Ta Ntchr, even Punt. Sometimes we would have visiting scholars from deep in the interior, far south of Kilimanjaro, the mountain of the moon. Every day was an exciting step into the past and future at the same time. I was at the top of my class in my peer group. The Mdw Ntchr, the divine words, was my favorite classes next to the Mentchu Medjay spiritual sciences. I knew more than fifty Ntchru by heart with all their meaning and attributes, and I could write them and draw them as well.

One day I was sitting on the Hapy Eteru bank studying my planets and crystals in relationship to the Ntchru when a cute young little girl, maybe two or three years younger than my age, came skipping by.

"Hey, you!" I yelled out. "I bet you don't know the fifth planet from Ra."

She gave me a silly look and then said, "Jupiter, ruled by Amen under the constellation of Khensu, under the element

4

of fire, vibrating with the color purple. A few of its stones are amethyst, topaz, lapis lazuli, and turquoise. Use herbs flowers like red raspberry, red clover if you are under that Heru vision. Always use lotus, sandalwood, and peppermint oils and incense. And the anatomy that is associated with the fifth planet and Khensu is the thigh and hip area, you silly boy. Everyone knows that. You must be from the star system Pleiadian." And then she skipped away.

Where was Pleiadian? I thought. I never heard of that place. Wow, who is that little girl, and who are her teachers? I never saw any girls in my classes. She was *nefer.*

* * *

After four years of intense training in the mysteries of Kemet, the Hem Ntchr Tepy summoned Mentchu-hotep and Kemet's greatest warrior, Jhutyms Ka-en-Heru, to meet him in the library at the Amen Temple of Ipet Asut. Spiritual Warrior Jhutyms was a Medjay warrior from Kash, and he was Kemet's most decorated warrior. He had led his Medjay troops into battle for Kemet over a dozen times and was never defeated. Mysterious legends surrounded the chief Medjay warrior Jhutyms Ka-en-Heru, and it is stated that when he runs in battle, he could not be heard and that he doesn't even leave footprints in the sand. At night he could not be seen, and you only knew he was there because he would leave behind a black Kheper (dung beetle) stone with his name on it. It is written that he has walked south to the end of the earth and back. He is from the direct bloodline of the legendary Nimrod, Memnon, and Annu. He is chief of all Medjay.

Kashite, like the one in the relief, swelled the ranks of
Kemet's armies and left a strong mark on its culture.

Medjay Jhutyms Ka-en-Heru came from a family of
spiritual warriors. His father was Chief Annu Aa of the Medjay
nation, and even his mother was a mighty warrior-priestess
of the Medjay nation before becoming the Mwt Nswt Wrt
(Great Royal Mother) Ukui. The Medjay culture was rooted in
harmonious nature; therefore, the warrior sciences developed
by the Medjay were based upon being in harmony with nature,
a symptomatic thought process. The Medjay warrior replicated
the movements of the best fighters in the animal world, as well
as the movements of celestial bodies in their orbits. Not only
could the Medjay warriors replicate the movements of animals,
but also they actually took on the spirit and sometimes
transformed into the animals. The Medjay did not separate
the physical aspect of combat from the mental and spiritual
realms. Through the use of sacred music, dance, invocations,
herbs, talismans, communion with special ancestors, and

forces of nature, the Medjay were able to create warriors unmatched in skill, strength, and bravery in the known world.

In Kemet, the word *Medjay* became synonymous with the words *royal guard* or *officer* or even *judge*. The Medjay warriors were highly skilled in both empty-handed and armed combat. They mastered a wide array of weapons including the spear, staff, mace, sword, bow and arrows, blowguns, various knives, animal claws, poisons, throwing sticks, manipulation of energy, and much more. It was said to become a Medjay warrior under Chief Medjay Jhutyms Ka-en-Heru and join his elite combat unit, you had to run through the desert twenty-six miles at night, but only after you survived his vigorous combat test of fighting ten regular combat warriors during the day and swimming across the Hapy Eteru at its widest point.

The crown prince Mentchu-hotep was honored to train under Kemet's greatest warrior, Chief Medjay Jhutyms Ka-en-Heru, but he was only a junior student, so he could not imagine why the Hem Ntchr Tepy Dagi wanted to meet with the both of them together.

After our formal greetings, the Hem Ntchr Tepy Dagi asked Medjay Jhutyms Ka-en-Heru how my training was going. I was actually shocked when he spoke clearly at great length in the Mdw Ntchr. He always spoke in riddles and only when absolutely necessary. In four years, I only heard him speak about a dozen times. At first I thought he only spoke in his native tongue from Barwat Upper Kash, but he actually spoke in several languages fluently, most I never heard of.

"He has great potential, great Neb of Ma'at. He is among the top students in the junior class. He learns quickly and has a keen mind for details. That is something you cannot teach my Neb of Ma'at," said the chief Medjay Jhutyms Ka-en-Heru.

I dared not look into their eyes because they were like the Ntchru, giants among men, and even though I was the crown prince, I was not worthy to be in their company. And I didn't want to show either of them how nervous I was.

"Very well," said the Hem Ntchr Tepy Dagi. He looked deep into my eyes, and then he said, "You will leave the morning after the new moon."

Leave for where? And what did this have to do with me? I thought. After an exchange of a few more words, the Medjay warrior Jhutyms Ka-en-Heru turned toward me and nodded his head, "Young prince, come closer. Can you see that seedling?"

"*Tiw*, yes," I said."

"Observe this plant pushing its way out of the darkness of *ta*, the soil, and into the light of Ra where it can express its full potential. This is going to be your journey into knowledge," he said as he turned and left quickly.

The Hem Ntchr Tepy Dagi turned and spoke to me, "Your father requested that not only should you learn to be articulate in thinking, speaking, writing, and fighting, but that you should learn who our allies are and who our enemies are and to be connected to nature as well as to the common people." He paused for a moment, then continued, "This is a great task, and there is no better teacher in this area of expertise than the chief Medjay Jhutyms Ka-en-Heru. Not only is he our greatest warrior, but also he is a scholar, linguist, and our most trusted diplomat, as well as being my teacher also. So for the next two years, you will be under his private tutelage. He will take you south to his homeland, Kash, and beyond to the tropical rain forest, and the great savannas, even the tallest mountains in all of Ta Netcher. It is important for you to know the source of the Ntchr Hapy, the greatest river in the world and the lifeline of Kemet, Ta Mry. It was because of this lack of knowledge of Hapy Eteru that our great nation Kemet, Sema Tawy was destroyed after the last golden age of the great Nswt Bety Shemsu Heru Nefer- Ka-Ra, Sa Ra Pepy.

"The way of the Medjay is a narrow gate, and the way is hard that leads to life and immortality. And those who find it are few. The gate opened by your ego is wide, and the way is easy that leads to destruction and death. And those who enter and follow are many. Your father, the Shemsu Heru, and the chief Medjay will lead you to the correct gate, but you must enter it, do you understand?"

I stepped forward with my left foot as I spoke, "Tiw, Dwa Ntchr!"

Mentchu-hotep, the crown prince

"We all journey to this world with full awareness of who we are and what our missions are. The key is to remember all that you have forgotten along the way. Become very watchful, careful, and aware of your thoughts, beliefs, and motives. Be determined that they are constructive and positive and designed to increase in harmony, peace, love, and spiritual

9

consciousness. These objectives can be achieved through the use of prayer, visualization, meditation, and consciousness. This will surely increase your spiritual stamina. Take excellent mental, physical, and spiritual notes and learn well from all your experiences. When you return, you will be tested on all you have learned. Go and greet your family, give much *mrr* [love] to your parents, your father and mother, for they are my family also, and to your little sister, Princess Neferu. You will leave in three days." There was no time for questions. The Hem Ntchr Tepy Dagi clapped his hands together, and I was escorted away quickly with my mind turning in circles.

* * *

"Mother, why must Mentchu-hotep leave Kemet when he is the crown prince and the smartest boy in his classes?"

"Because he is thirteen years old, Neferu, it is time for him to learn the way of the warrior, and only a warrior can teach a person to be a warrior."

"But I watch him train, Mother, every day. He has even taught me how to fight. I don't understand why he can't learn to be a warrior in Kemet. Aren't our Kemet warriors great?"

"*Tiw*, yes, Neferu, our Kemet warriors are great, but like his great- grandfather whom he is named after, he is to become a Medjay warrior- priest. The Medjay come from Ta Ntchr beyond Kash in the south."

"I want to go too then. Can I be Medjay? I'm named after my great- grandmother from the south who was a Medjay warrior woman."

"Listen carefully, Neferu, your place, our place is here."

"No, my place is beside Mentchu-hotep. I saw it in a dream, Mother, as clear as day! You know I have the power of vision, Mother."

"*Tiw*, little Neferu, and you shall be by his side because we are the throne makers. Our function as the royal women is to transmit rulership through the female line. While every Kemet princess of the royal house was born Hemet Nswt and bore the title and dignities of the office from the day of her birth, your brother Mentchu-hotep only acquires them at his coronation, and he can only do so only by becoming the consort of the royal princess. But first, little royal princess, you must learn how to be the high priestess of Het Heru."

"He told me, Mother, that I was his lotus flower forever. Can I just marry him now?"

"You have forgotten your way, little one, and your purpose, now you want to sit on the bottom of the mat."

* * *

At high noon, Mentchu-hotep entered his parent's royal palace, and Neferu lit up like a candle as she ran and jumped into his arms.

"Why do you have to go? I miss you, Brother, I miss you so much." He sat her down in one of the royal chairs.

"Neferu, I must leave tomorrow and start my journey of knowledge, a journey into the life of a Medjay warrior. I need your prayers and strength to help me, for I am like an ant standing next to Kilimanjaro when I am in his presence. He is the chief of all Medjay, Jhutyms Ka- en-Heru. Are you going to help me?"

11

"Ok, but you must write me every day," she said.

"Neferu, you know I can't write you every day, I will be training hard to be a Medjay."

"Well, every other day."

"I will write when I can and send you gifts from all the lands that I visit."

Neferu grabbed him around his shoulders. "You promise." "*Tiw*, I promise."

Neferu got very serious for a moment, "That Jhutyms Ka-en-Heru is scary. I looked into his eyes once, and I saw stars and planets from another solar system, and a strange energy I have never felt before."

And then she whispers in Mentchu-hotep's ear, "I don't think he's from this planet," with a very serious look on her face.

"Listen, my little lotus flower, I want you to train very hard while I am gone. I need a warrior-princess by my side."

"*Tiw*, I can already beat up everyone in my class." She threw several kicks and punches in the air.

"Now I told you about beating people up, plus your mother, the Hmt Nswt Wrt, will be angry."

"You promise."

"Well, all right. I promise."

"Can I write you and tell you about my new friend? She is from Napata. She is smart, very pretty, and she can fight too. Her brother is a Medjay also. I will train with her."

Mentchu-hotep picked up his little sister in his arms and kissed her on the forehead.

"Remember, you are my little blooming lotus flower," pointing his

finger at her nose.

"You remember," pointing back at him. "You are my golden crown prince."

They both laughed. The Nswt Hemet Wrt Iah, his mother, entered the room.

"I heard that. No fighting, little girl."

"Mother, I will miss your teachings and your guidance."

"Just remember this, my son Mentchu-hotep, even if you don't know the answer, spirit knows, even if you don't know the reason, spirit knows. In all matters and in all things, allow your life to be guided by the Divine Spirit. The Divine Spirit is the truth, and the truth is the truth whether you understand and agree with it or not. The divine truth is not subject to your interpretation. You just follow it, do you understand?"

"Tiw."

"The proper and greatest way to learn is to acquire learning directly from nature. When the Divine Spirit is guiding you, no formal studies are necessary. You will be fine, son. The mystery of life isn't a problem to solve but a reality to experience." She looked at her growing son with so much pride. "Open your heart to the beauty in life, and your life will reflect that beauty in your heart. Remember, my son, a peaceful heart within makes beauty without."

"*Tiw*, yes, Mother, I will remember."

The first year and a half of my trip, I spent in great pain. Before one group of muscles could recover, another set was sore or swollen or both. I had to admit, I learned a lot about herbology: What plant cured what pain and what herb relaxed what part of the human body. What group of herbs helped you handle stress? What mixture of herbs could put you to sleep? My feet were always in agony. I learned what plants were great muscle relaxers. The great Medjay even taught me how to massage myself, relaxing almost any part of the body. I walked or ran enough for four lifetimes. He taught me how to make my own shoes because I was wearing out a pair every month. He only wore shoes at special occasions, and the lightness of his steps was unbelievable. We ran up mountains, down valleys, across savannas, in the desert—we even ran in the rain and in water. I saw Medjay Jhutyms Ka-en-Heru run down a desert rabbit—unbelievable!—and then he apologized to the rabbit and asked for its forgiveness and just let it go. He found food that animals couldn't find. Once we were in the desert with no water, he drank his urine. I couldn't do that, so he caught a snake and made me drink its blood, then he turned the snakeskin into a canteen and tied it around my arm.

Then he said, "When we take a life, we must always ask for forgiveness, and we must never waste valuable energy."

That night he asked me, "Are you listening to life? Are you listening to the subtle messages contained in every condition, situation, and relationship in your life right now? Listen to what life is saying. Then commit to make the adjustments that are needed. Remember, you are not a person, you just experience that you are. You are a divine spirit." The last six months of our journey, I practiced a lot of animal fighting forms, and he gave me a great foundation of the spear, long pole, bow and arrow, and medium sword–fighting techniques. Meditation was also part of our everyday routine, and only during the last three months did I start to get the hang of it. The rest of the time, I think I was in too much pain to quiet my mind. Once, we were freezing—no, correction—I was freezing on top of Kilimanjaro, the tallest mountain in all our land, when Medjay Jhutyms Ka-en-Heru felt something was wrong. He said it was a disturbance in the force.

While during his meditation, "It's your family, I can feel their pain," he said. He sent his great falcon messenger bird back to Kemet with a note, and in about three days' time, the great falcon returned with a note that my mother's brother's son, the mayor of Iwn, had had a stroke but was recovering nicely. If the great Medjay could feel my family thousands of miles away through meditation, that was enough to make a believer out of me. From that day on, I have been faithful with my meditation.

The great Medjay said to me, "The sacred traditions of the Medjay insist that by connecting with nature, we connect not only with the ancestors and the Ntchru, we also connect with the deepest, most ancient part of ourselves, the Divine Spirit. To the quiet mind, all things are possible. Everything is connected. Everything is related. Everything is *one*. A person's worldly experience is an optical delusion of their consciousness created by the ego. We must always focus on the *one*, never the symbols but only the symptoms."

Marching Medjay warriors from Kash and Kemet
with bows and arrows and spears.

When the crown prince Mentchu-hotep and the chief Medjay spiritual warrior Jhutyms Ka-en-Heru returned to Kemet after nearly two and a half years, they were greeted with a grand reception. One hundred Medjay warriors from Chief Medjay Jhutyms Ka-en-Heru's special forces led the parade as they entered the great temple of Amen at Ipet Asut. There the Nswt Intef-sa-Ra and the Hemet Nswt Wrt Iah along with the Hem Ntchr Tepy Dagi and several other high priests and priestesses greeted them. That day there was a great feast with much dancing and music, and to highlight the evening, the visiting Medjay warriors from Jhutyms Ka-en-Heru's own village in Kash gave an unbelievable Mentchu Medjay combat demonstration. Several Medjay warriors did forms of the elements—fire, earth, wind, and water—and they seemed to have changed the weather while a small group of Medjay medju did several animal forms and then seemed to transform back in forth from human to animal to human before your very eyes.

We all were stunned by their skills. They bent knives and swords with their bodies, caught arrows out of the air, ate fire without being burned, danced on glass without being cut, and the highlight before the temple dancers were three matches between three Asiatic masters versus three Medjay warriors.

The drums rolled and roared like a mighty lion, and the first match began. A huge Asiatic master about six feet four, weighing well over three hundred pounds charged the first Medjay warrior. The Medjay leaped over his head, landing behind him, and when the Asiatic turned around, he was swept to the ground with a spinning wheel sweep. The Asiatic hit the ground with a great thud. But he bounced up quickly, showing great speed for such a big man. The crowd roared. This time the Asiatic pulled out his sword, and the Medjay laughed. The huge warrior swung his sword toward the Medjay head, but he ducked under the sword to deliver a powerful blow to the Asiatic warrior's groin. The Asiatic warrior fell to his knees, and by this time, the Medjay had stripped the sword from his hand and grabbed him around his neck into a deadly headlock. And within seconds, the Medjay had put the huge Asiatic warrior to sleep. The crowd roared with applause as the huge Asiatic warrior lay out cold in the heat of the arena. Within seconds, a group of Kemet healers, all dressed in white robes, came to the fallen warrior's aid. The Asiatic warrior was attended to and was revitalized by the Kemetic healers, and after a few minutes, they helped him off the courtyard. The Kemet crowd cheered the Asian's recovery.

The second match was met with an even greater roar from the crowd for it was Chief Medjay Jhutyms Ka-en-Heru's son, a champion in his own homeland, Kash. The Asiatic master entered with a spear and two knives around his side, but the Medjay Ka-en-Jhutyms chose only to use his bare hands even though he was a master of many weapons. The Medjay warrior knelt before his father, the greatest champion in all of Kemet, then to the Hem Ntchr Tepy and the royal court and then saluted his Asiatic opponent. The Asiatic master bowed back, and then the match began. They both moved slowly at first as they circled each other. Finally, the Asiatic master lunged his spear toward the Medjay's chest, but the Medjay turned sideways, evading contact, then broke the spear in half with a mighty blow, catching the spearpoint half in his right hand. The whole crowd stood on its feet. The Medjay blocked the remaining back half of the spear with his left hand as he cartwheeled in the air over the Asiatic's head and then using the spear tip and thrusting it through the Asiatic's arm, holding onto the broken spear. And before the Asiatic could cry out from the pain, the Medjay had taken one of his knives from his waist and held it to his throat. This match was over, and the Asiatic master feel to his knees, thanking the Medjay for sparing his life. The crowed stood again with a roaring applause. Again the Kemetic healers came to attend to the wounded Asiatic master as they helped him off the courtyard with the spear tip still sticking through his arm. The crowd got very silent for the third match. They had not seen anything like this before. The Asiatic warrior wore a large black bear suit over his head, shoulders, and chest with only part of his face out. His huge arms and legs were covered with tattoos, and he stood maybe seven feet tall with a huge wooden club in his right hand and bear claws in the left. He held up his club and growled at the crowd of shocked onlookers. Finally, the third Medjay warrior appeared, small but very muscular, maybe five feet nine with a bald head and vey dark complexion, glowing black in the hot but brilliant Kemet sun. He humbly bowed before the royal court, and the Hem Ntchr Tepy of the Amen temple stood up because this warrior Medjay was the high priest Hem Ntchr Tepy of the great temple of Amen in Kash in the great city of Barwat, one of his greatest pupils. You could hear the crowd murmuring. Maybe this was a mismatch for surely this wild beast looked almost invisible as he beat on his hairy chest, growling at the Medjay warrior. But the Medjay just smiled as he bowed toward the Asiatic beast. The gong sounded, and the match began. The Asiatic beast charged the Medjay, swirling his huge club in the air, but the Medjay did not move. The beast swung his mighty club toward the Medjay's head, but without blocking, the Medjay stepped into the eye of the storm. And with one quick blow to the throat of the beast, it stopped him in his tracks. His second blow following so quickly, almost unseen by the naked eye, was upward to the nose of the beast. The beast fell slowly backward like a giant tree in slow motion, but he was dead before he could hit the ground. The crowd stood in silence and in disbelief for a moment, and then after the royal court stood and clapped, the crowed joined in with a roaring applause as they dragged the Asiatic beast's body off the courtyard. This would be the talk of the city for years to come for the legendary Medjay warriors had firmly etched out a permanent place in the Mentchu combat arts history for millenniums to come.

The young prince sat at the royalcourt table next to Chief Medjay Warrior Jhutyms Ka-en-Heru on his right and the Hem Ntchr Tepy Dagi of Ipet Asut on his left. His head was still spinning in awe at what he had just witnessed. He thought, *I am not worthy of being here with these giants among men and women who have earned great titles and who have proven themselves in battle amongst their enemies.* He could see his great father, Nswt Intef-sa-Ra, and his mother, the Hemet Nswt Wrt Iah, staring and his little sister waving and smiling at him with pride that he did not deserve.

His mother smiled at him as she said, "And you've grown at least six inches, my son, you will be tall like your great-grandfather Shemsu Heru Mentchu-hotep." He ate his food slowly and silently, barely hearing or seeing the great Kashite and Kemet dancers, drummers, and musicians in the background. But he was only thinking of his diminutive skills compared to what he had just witnessed. But most of all, he avoided looking at his little sister who thought he was powerful like Ra.

Royal banquet

The next morning, Mentchu-hotep rose with Ra. He could only think about the challenge that lay ahead of him. After the prince had washed, he prayed in silent meditation at the doorway of the Holy of Holies for a long time before going to practice his Mentchu combat arts. After about an hour of serious training, he washed again and ate breakfast. He thought about his journey of a lifetime with Kemet's greatest warrior, Chief Medjay Jhutyms Ka-en-Heru. He thought about the Medjay knowledge of herbs and medicines, crystals and stones, and a host of healing arts. How he could identify almost every bird, animal, and insect on their journey.

I remember him saying to me one evening after hunting down a lion, "We, the Medjay, do not start from the premise that we are higher than the rest of creation on earth. The Emerald Tablets tell us that in ancient times, some animals and birds spoke the language of human beings and some human beings spoke the languages of animals and birds through pure thought. To the ancient mind of the Medjay, animals, plants, and humans were parts of one large earthly family. And we can become one with it." Now this oneness, I'm still trying to understand.

Each and every morning before practice, he read from the sacred text in Mdw Ntchr of knowing the creation of Ra, memorizing whole chapters by heart.

At fifteen years, how can I compete with that? I thought. *I better start training again right now. I'm wasting precious time,* I thought. At noontime, the great Medjay Jhutyms Ka-en-Heru came for me. Without saying a word, I followed him to the library meeting room where the Hem Ntchr Tepy Dagi was already waiting. On the outside, I seemed calm, but inside I was spinning around in circles. *I hope I don't embarrass my family and myself,* I thought.

After we all gave praise to the Ntchru and greeted each other, then the Hem Ntchr Tepy stood before a sacred altar for Amen-Ra. He was carrying a very fancy bowl of water with the shape of a ram's head made of gold and silver and a small tree inside a planter with the face of Het Heru on it. He stepped forward with his left leg and his left hand open in the Ma'at posture and then closed his eyes and began the libation. We followed each of his postures:

Hem Ntchr Tepy: In the name of the Nswt of the Ntchru Amen-Ra, the hidden one, the almighty force, the Ntchr of breath and life. Great Amen-Ra, who was self-produced at the beginning of time, self-existent, almighty, and eternal force, which created all the Ntchru and gave form to all things. Amen, you are the unseen and unseenable creative force that is spirit and all thoughts. Ra, you are the Ntchr of light and victory, of protection, and of immeasurable power. You are the seen force of the universe manifested by the sun. Ra, you are the energy that allows light to shine. You are Kheper in the morning, Ra at noon, and Atum, the complete one, in the evening. As Amen-Ra, you have no equal. You are the sun that keeps us warm, the spirit that offers us life. You mark the cycle of day and night, months and years, centuries and millennia. You are eternal. We ask Amen-Ra to be with us, to strengthen us, and to give us vision for a great Kemet future.

Response: Dwa! *As the Hem Ntchr Tepy poured water into the tree.*

Hem Ntchr Tepy: *This time the left leg still remained forward, but his hands rose in the Ka posture, and we followed.* In the name of the great Ntchru, the cosmic and celestial Ntchru, that aid Amen-Ra in the maintenance and general operation of the universe. These Ntchru are laws and principles of creation and act as the managers of all existence for all life known and unknown. In the name of the Duat Ntchru, they represent the intermediate plane. These Ntchru are realms of light that are responsible for transformation between the spiritual and the physical material worlds and to the Terrestrial Ntchru, and they represent nature and the natural functions of things on our planet. We ask these Ntchru to be with us, to strengthen us, and to give us vision for a great Kemet future.

Response: Dwa! *As the Hem Ntchr Tepy poured water into the tree.*

Hem Ntchr Tepy: *This time only his left hand rose in the air with his right hand across his chest, but the left foot still remained forward, and we followed.* In the name of the first great *remtch* (original humans), who began the march of humanity and civilization, who were guided by Jhuty, Ma'at, and Seshat, and who came out of the womb of the mother of creation—Mwt, Het Heru, Sekhmet. We ask the great mother Ntchru, mistress of the universal feminist energies to be with us, to strengthen us, and to give us vision for a great Kemet future.

Response: Dwa! *As the Hem Ntchr Tepy poured water into the tree.*

Hem Ntchr Tepy: *This time he knelt down on one knee, his right knee, left hand up and right hand across the chest, and we followed.* In the name of the first great *remtch* leaders who began the march of humanity and civilization— Asar, Aset, and Heru— and to the Khemmennu Ntchru.

The Khemmennu Ntchru were eight deities who were the basis of the Kemet's creation myth during the second golden age. They were primarily worshipped in Khemmennu, but their aspects of the creation were combined in other areas with existing myths. Each one is a member of a masculine-feminine pair, and each pair represents an aspect of the primordial chaos out of which the world was created. They all came into being at the same time. Nun and Nanuet represent the primordial seas, Kuk and Kauker represents the infinite darkness, Hu and Huhet represents empty space, and Amen and Amenunet represent quintessence or the secret powers of creation.

The Ntchru Khemmennu at Khemmennu was led by Jhuty. In the name of the great triad of Waset—Amen, Mwt, and Khensu—to the great triad in Kash, Khnum, Anuket, and Satet, to the great triad in the north—Ptah, Sekhmet, and Nefer-Atum—and the great triad of the south here in

Waset—Asr, Ast and Heru. We ask these Ntchru to be with us, to strengthen us, and to give us vision for a great Kemet future.

Response: Dwa! *As the Hem Ntchr Tepy poured water into the tree.*

Hem Ntchr Tepy: *Now he knelt on both knees with his hands crossed like Asr, and we followed.* In the name of the first great remtch and Kemetyu leaders who began civilization in the Hapy Valley, establishing their high culture and building their temples, great monuments, pyramids, and tombs to the Ntchru and great human spirits. We ask these great remtch and Kemetyu like Imhotep and Ptah-hotep and the best of our ancestors' great spirits to be with us, to strengthen us, and to give us vision for a great Kemet future.

Response: Dwa! *As the Hem Ntchr Tepy poured water into the tree.*

Hem Ntchr Tepy: *This time he bent his head forward, touching his forehead to the ground with both knees bent in prayer, and we followed.* In the name of Shemsu Heru who came from the south to Kemet; from Kash, Ta-Sety, Punt, Ta Khuy, Ta Ntchr; from the three mountains of the moon; and beyond where the Heru Bess dwells who guided and taught the Shemsu Heru hear in Kemet like Heru Narmer, Heru Aha, Heru Djer, Heru Djet, Heru Den, Heru Anedjib, Heru Semerkhet, Heru Qa'a, Heru Hotepsekhemwy, Heru NebRa, Heru Nynetchr, Heru Set- peribsen, Heru Khasekhemwy, Heru Sanakhte, Heru Netchrikhet, Heru Sekhemkhet, Heru Khaba, Heru Huni, Heru Snefru, Heru Khufu, Heru DjedefRa, Heru KhafRa, Heru MenkauRa, Heru Shepseskaf,

Heru Userkaf, Heru SahuRa, Heru NeferifkaRa, Heru ShepseskaRa, Heru NeferefRa, Heru NiuserRa, Heru Menkauheru, Heru DjedkaRa, Heru Unas, Heru Teti, Heru Pepy, Heru MerenRa, Heru Pepy NeferkaRa, Heru WadjkaRa, Heru MeryibRa, Heru MerykaRa, Heru KaneferRa, Heru QakaRa,

Heru NebkauRa, and our beloved Heru Sehertawy-Sa Ra Intef. We ask these great Shemsu Heru to be with us, to strengthen us, and to give us vision for a great Kemet future.

Response: Dwa! Dwa! Dwaaaaaaaaaa! *As he poured the last of the water from the bowl into the tree.*

"You may be seated," spoke the Hem Netcher Tepy Dagi as we rose from our knees to sit in the large comfortable chairs in the library. I was blown away again as he recited from memory all the Shemsu Heru since the reunification of ancient Kemet under Shemsu Heru Narmer. That's almost two thousand years of our story.

I thought, *one day I will be asked to do that very same libation. Wow, I got work to do.*

The high priest spoke again, "The great spiritual warrior, Chief Medjay Jhutyms Ka-en-Heru, said he was pleased with your progress as a junior student, but you are still not ready to be a Medjay warrior."

I thought, *no joking, was that an understatement? I'm not even worthy to hold their weapons.*

The Hem Ntchr Tepy Dagi spoke again, "I want you to think clearly before you speak. You have trained personally with possibly the greatest known warrior in the world, traveled to places most people cannot even dream about, spoken with kings and heads of state. I even understand that you saw Medjay Jhutyms wrestle a crocodile and slit its throat before breaking his jaws."

I thought back to that battle, and it was inhuman. He fought like one of the Ntchru, not a human being. Chief Medjay Jhutyms Ka-en- Heru pulled the crocodile under the water, slit its throat, and tied his mouth shut. Then after killing it, he dragged the giant crocodile out of the water and made both of us handbags and belts out of its skin and then feed the meat to the natives. *They will remember and talk about that for another hundred years*, I thought.

He spoke again, "When you entered the great tropical rain forest in the south and then walked through the great savannas of the east and even slept on top of the world at the mountains of the moon, what did you feel, hear, and see?"

I thought, *He has to be joking with me. He wants me to put that into words?* I paused to collect my thoughts, then I took a deep breath before speaking.

"Hem Ntchr Tepy," I replied, "first I felt it a great honor to even walk in the footsteps of the great Medjay warrior Jhutyms Ka-en-Heru when I could find his footsteps. He did many things that were totally incomprehensible to the human mind and could not be duplicated by any human being. He is truly Ntchr-like! I have gained great knowledge through him of herbs and the natural plant life, what is eatable and what to be left alone. He taught me to listen with my heart. It is the heart that sees always before the head can see. Words are the domain of the linear mind. Only the heart can hear the language of plants. I gained a great knowledge of the animals and birds, and I even learned how to speak or make the sounds like a few. I had a hard time adjusting to the various temperature changes from the desert to the tropical rain forest to the freezing cold mountaintops. It was even difficult swimming in the ice-cold waters of Hapy. None of these seem to affect the Medjay one little bit. As far as dealing with rulers and diplomats, the Medjay taught me that most of them are greedy and valueless, and they are symbolic thinkers ruled by superstitions and mythology. They use Ma'at only to their advantage, so he taught me to listen far more than I speak, for if you listen carefully, feed their ego, they will tell you all that you need to know. As far as the sounds and sights of nature, I could hear the great falcon call, the leaves rustling in the wind as ibises and cranes flew over our heads. I could hear the peaceful sounds of running water or its mighty thunder of its waves. I hear the night roar of the lion, the rumble of zebra herds and wildebeest, and even the chatter of baboons as they gave praise to the sun, Ra, as it rose in the morning sky."

When the young prince Mentchu-hotep finished, the Hem Ntchr Tepy Dagi asked, "What else did you learn from the great Medjay warrior Jhutyms Ka-en-Heru, your spiritual guide?"

The young prince Mentchu-hotep replied, "He did not speak much, only in riddles that mostly went over my head. Pain seemed to be his favorite lesson, how to inflict pain from many positions. These various positions he called postures and animal stances. We stood in Ulimwengo, Ka, Ma'at, and Heru Djed every day for hours. We sat in Kukaa, laid in the Asarian posture for days, silent. We watched and imitated various animals, at least I did, and I think he transformed into some of them. I couldn't tell the Medjay from the natural animals after a while, and that's not a good feeling. I learned to fight like the crane, baboon, lion, the black panther, the falcon, the cobra, and the Hapy crocodile."

When the young prince finished this time, the great Medjay Jhutyms Ka-en-Heru and the Hem Ntchr Tepy stood up and walked outside the library room, talking to each other about what they had just heard. The prince thought, *Was I that bad? Actually, I thought I did pretty well for a youth.* Only the Hem Ntchr Tepy returned to the room, and it looked like the Medjay vanished in thin air.

The Hem Ntchr Tepy Dagi placed his hand on the young prince's shoulder and spoke. "You have missed some of the great Medjay's most important lessons. We will send two of his most trusted Medjay warriors with you back up south to the land of our sacred ancestors, back to Kash, Punt, Ta Khuy, Ta Ntchr, and to the mountains of the moon again. This time you must dig deeper into the spirit of the great Medjay Jhutyms Ka-en-Heru's lessons."

The prince was puzzled by the Hem Ntchr Tepy's request. Had he not discerned every sound already? Hadn't he endured enough pain for two lifetimes? Is this what his father wanted him to learn?

The Hem Ntchr Tepy Dagi spoke again, "Something that you must always remember is that by keeping you looking outside yourself for answers, the ego prevents you from really looking at its thought system. You think you are your body, so you're not looking at how it protects the illusions.

"You are an excellent student of the Mdw Ntchr, and you must study the great Medjay's teachings like you study the Mdw Ntchr. It is the marriage of the soul with nature that makes the intellect fruitful, which gives birth to imagination.

"Listen carefully, each letter in the Mdw Ntchr alphabet pictorially is a symbol of a certain sound during a certain state of being, and that sound could change if the conditions change. This symbol is understood symbolically. Each letter also represents a number, and each number represents a completely new set of mental, physical, and spiritual properties. So the simple alphabet has multilevels of meanings based upon your level of understanding. Are you beginning to see this picture? A letter could be a sound, but that sound is not fixed. It can change or it could be a word or it could be a hidden code of numbers expressing a spiritual concept. And just like the Mdw Ntchr, syllabic signs can take four different meanings, so can a move in the Mentchu Medjay combat system."

"*Tiw*, yes, Great Teacher. I'm beginning to understand the concepts. I've been thinking lineal and symbolic, but the teachings are organic, holistic and multidimensional, and symptomatic," I said.

"Keep that thought as you return on your new journey, that just like a Mdw Ntchr symbol must be understood symptomatically can have up to four different possibilities, so can each lesson in life. You have the concrete meaning—it is what it is, the abstract meaning or the function of a thing, and then there is a spiritual meaning, and only for the initiate, there is the numerical esoteric meaning."

The prince knelt down on one knee and spoke, "I shall try harder my Neb, and I can see now what the great Medjay was trying to explain to me when he taught the five elements of fire, earth, water, air, and spirit that exist within each technique. He said that the movements were organic and alive. Yet the predictability was that it was unpredictable. Yes, each stance or posture or animal, just like the Mdw Ntchr, had infinite possibilities that explained the probability of movement mentally, physically, and spiritually. I will not let you down, and I pray that the great Medjay Jhutyms Ka-en-Heru will forgive me. I will not let him down again, and I must not let my father and mother or my little sister, Neferu, down for I will be worthy one day to be Shemsu Heru Nswt Bety."

CHAPTER 2

THE RETURN, NEW BEGINNINGS

I rose before Ra every day for the next three months, practicing all my Ma'at Akhu Ba ankh drills and forms. These were meditation and breathing forms along with stretching drills that I had learned from the mighty Medjay warrior Jhutyms Ka-en-Heru. I remembered asking the chief Medjay, how does one know the self and how can you and my parents know me better than I do?

First of all, the chief Medjay said, "Your self does not belong to you. What you think is you are part of a collective pool of energy in which a portion has been loaned to you as an investment toward the expansion of your gifts to the world in which we are part of. He went on to say, "The nature of self is to understand the nature of the Ntchru. The eyes with which we see the Ntchru are the same eyes with which the Ntchru see us. Therefore, it is important for us to learn to see with our hearts and our minds for it is only with the heart, an aspect of our minds, that one can see righteously. What is essential is invisible to the eye. Seeing is feeling with the spirit, and when one feels with one's heart, it will show you that the nature of the Ntchr is a circle of which the center is everything. And the

31

circumference is a reflection of the center. The self, which you think is the I am is only the heart, which is the spirit, which is the one, which is everything. And the body is an illusion."

I stood in Ulimwengo for thirty minutes in a standing meditation drill, contemplating these ideas and then one hour of animal fighting followed by the five elements—earth, water, air, fire, and ether—and then a water break followed by one more hour of weapon training. Each Medjay had to master five different weapons of their choice. And you trained with each weapon like it was a life-and-death situation, and it was your only savior.

I felt I was making some real progress. I was flowing through my moves without thinking about them. I could feel that I had much more control over my breathing, and I was told countless times that breathing was the key of self-mastery. When I looked up, Medjay Jhutyms Ka- en-Heru was standing next to me. I did not jump or act startled, even though I was, because I was facing the door. And the walls are twelve feet high with no other entrance. It's like he just appeared in thin air.

"*Nefer*," he said in a very calm voice, "you are making good progress. But your parents are worried about you spending so much time alone and practicing day and night."

"Great Neb Medjay Jhutyms Ka-en-Heru, I have been feeling disconnected with an emptiness like I let everyone down since my return. I just wanted to work harder and be better."

"First of all, you let no one down. You survived two and a half years training with me. That is a great accomplishment. And your family is very proud of you. The people of Kemet are extremely proud of you. Remember, young Crown Prince, you are never alone. In an attempt to let us know we are not alone, countless spirits call upon us from the depths of our bones. These are what we call our spirit allies. They have been with us before our physical journey and continue to be with us during this life cycle. It is important to realize that when we feel something is missing in our life, when we feel disconnected or displaced, these feelings are signs for us to repair our connection with the Divine Spirit. Remember, the Divine Spirit is not in the world. How can it be in a world that isn't there? The Divine Spirit is in your mind. That's where both the problem and the answer are."

The chief Medjay Jhutyms Ka-en-Heru smiled before speaking, "Your new training will start tomorrow, so go and visit your family before you leave."

That evening after dinner, I entered my father's study. I could hear him giving praise to the Ntchr Khnum, Neb of Ta-Sety. When he saw me, he paused and met me in the doorway.

"Enter, my son." As we embraced for a long minute without any words, finally he spoke, "I saw the chief Medjay Jhutyms Ka-en-Heru, and he explained to me his plans. And I gave him my full gratitude and support. Some things I know you don't understand right now, son, but you will. Our intentions should always be to transmit the higher spiritual energies and meaning of life. All the great Nswt Bety's, masters, priests, and divine teachers of the past and present have placed great emphasis upon the quality of our thoughts. They have demonstrated throughout their teachings how thought can and does modify our environment and experiences. Awareness of our thoughts must come first, followed by discipline of our routine thinking. Son, I am so very proud of you, and I know it is the discipline that is your challenge right now that's why we have not seen much of you. Your mother and I understand,

33

but your little sister, Neferu, is not taking it so well. But she is growing fast also, speak to her before you leave."

I stared at my father for a long while, and I thought, *If I could just be half the ruler he is, I would be pleased.*

Neferu and I walked in the sacred garden of Het Heru with only the stars watching over us. Without talking, we could feel each other's thoughts. Thoughts of compassion can console the heavy heart when words cannot be found or are inadequate. Thoughts of a caring and loving nature can inspire, motivate, protect, and provide a sense of security because they touch the soul and are in harmony with the creative urges and purpose of the soul and the universe.

"I know you need me to be strong, my prince, but being without you is my greatest challenge. And just when I thought Amen-Ra had brought you back to me safely, you are snatched away again."

I held her hands but no words came out; only tears trickled slowly down my face.

Neferu spoke again, "Father has explained to me your mission and what you must do, and I promise to love and support you for you are my life."

We hugged in silence for a long time. I kissed her on the forehead and spoke, "The higher self, the divine mind within each of us, I must learn how to let it guide my thoughts, my reasoning, and my actions. We are destined, Neferu, to become creators of peace and harmony. We must strengthen our ability to love compassionately and unconditionally. I promise to return to you with a greater spirit and a greater love."

About two hours after sunrise the next day, two Medjay warriors stood at my doorway, and I recognized them both. They had fought the foreign warriors from Asia at the reception of our return. The taller of the two was from Kemet, the city of Abu, and he was one of Medjay Jhutyms Ka-en-Heru's elite Medjay warriors. And the second Medjay I could never forget for he is the son of Kemet's greatest warrior, Chief Medjay Jhutyms Ka-en-Heru, and he is from Barwat, the capital of Meroe in Kash.

Were these warriors my escorts? I don't think so, I thought. *They must be here to take me to my escorts or to another meeting.*

"Dwa, young Prince Mentchu-hotep," they both spoke as one voice.

The elder of the two Medjay spoke, "I am Medjay Sia-en-hotep of Abu, and this is a great Medjay warrior from Kash, Medjay Ka-en- Jhutyms from Barwat, we have come to guide you on your journey and initiation into the Medjay nation. We will return in two hours. Pack very light, our journey is long. And we naturally posses all that we need."

They bowed, placing one hand in the other, backed away and then left swiftly. *Wow,* I thought, *this is nefer, now this idea is great. I can train with other human beings, not the Ntchru.*

Two hours later, we boarded a small royal Heru boat with the designs of Heru on the sails. And in the front and back of the boat, it was painted red, black, and green and was built for speed. Two other Medjay onboard did the rowing.

"This is Medjay Ni-Sobek and Medjay Bennu Henenu from Barwat, Kash. They will be part of your training team this complete journey."

Great, I thought, *they were young men maybe five or six years my senior.* "We will stop at the sacred temple of Heru in the city of Behdet to pay our respects and to receive their blessings, then we will stop only to make deliveries at the sacred temples of Ta Sna and Djeba. Then we will travel to the twin temple of Nebet. There we will pick up supplies in the market place before moving on to Abu. At Abu, we will spend two months at one of our Medjay camps."

* * *

As we were traveling upstream for about a two-hour journey, no one said a word the entire trip. The two young Medjay rowed the whole two hours without a break, and they never seemed to tire. I was tired watching them. The view was awesome with the sun glowing in our faces. I have taken this journey many times with my parents, but today everything seemed more special, from this swift royal Heru boat and the Medjay warriors onboard. I felt a sense of serenity along the banks of Hapy Eteru, farmers attending their crops, women gathering water, children playing in the tall grasses, several fishermen casting their nets, smoke coming from rooftops, and water buffalos wadding in the water.

Did I recall Medjay Sia-en-hotep saying that I was going through the Medjay initiation? I thought, *Wow, my dream may come true after all if I live through it.*

"We are here" spoke Medjay Sia-en-hotep. "Medjay Ni-Sobek will board first and prepare our way."

When we docked, the two Medjay moved swiftly, one tied the Heru boat down while the other ran at top speed up the hill and vanished. When he returned after only a short time, several wab priests dressed in long white robes and completely bald-headed came and greeted us by dropping on one knee and bowing their heads in respect. Then they escorted us into the temple. Medjay Bennu Henenu stayed behind to guard our royal boat. At the royal entrance of the temple, we bathed with beautiful bowls all decorated with Behdet in the Mdw Ntchr all over them. *Very nice touch,* I thought. When we entered the second hall, we were met by two priests dressed in long gold-and-white robes. They escorted us into Behdet's sacred library room. Four beautiful women all dressed in long white robes brought us two pitchers of limewater and two beautiful decorated bowls of fruit. They bowed and placed one hand inside the other and then backed away and exited quickly.

"Please rest a moment, the Hem Ntchr Tepy will greet you shortly," one of the Hem Ntchr priest said as he left the room. My eyes searched the room, and there was Mdw Ntchr (divine writing of wise words) on every wall from top to bottom. On one wall, Heru and Enpu were giving life to the Nswt Bety at Behdet.

The other Hem Ntchr priest spoke, "You recognize this room, young prince?"

"*Tiw,* yes, it's one of my favorites," I said. At that moment, the Hem Sem Tepy entered, and we all stood up and bowed our heads with one hand inside the other.

"Please sit," the Hem Sem Tepy said. "I am your servant. And, young Prince Mentchu-hotep, I was chosen by your father, Shemsu Heru Nswt Intef-sa-Ra Nakhet Neb-Tep-Nefer. My duty is to serve the people in this village through mental, physical, and spiritual guidance, teach and develop community scribes, and maintain Ma'at. I am a cultural and spiritual custodian, and I am honored that you stopped here on your journey."

"Thank you for receiving us with such a short notice. We are truly guided by Amen-Ra under the orders of the Hem Ntchr Tepy Dagi of Ipet Asut in Waset," spoke Medjay Sia-en-hotep.

We all said in harmony, "Dwa Ntchr." The Hem Ntchr Tepy himself guided us around the temple with singing choir girls in the background, chanting hymns to Heru of Behdet. They had magnificent voices besides being stunningly beautiful.

As we walked back to our boat, the priest and singing girls followed us, and I stumbled a few times, trying to keep my concentration on my mission. But these girls had me hypnotized. The other Medjay seemed not to hear them or see them. When we arrived at our boat, greetings were given to the priest, and we all knelt. Then we were directed to enter Hapy, the great Eteru (river), as we held hands while the Hem Sem Tepy gave us a prayer, "Adorations to Hapy, hail to you, great Hapy. Come to Kemet! Come and nourish us. Come with your ancient secrets to which your followers sing. Hapy that floods the fields that Ra has made to nourish all who thirst, let's drink your magical waters, Neb of awe, he who controls both sky and earth, conqueror of the two lands, gives bounty to the rich and to the poor, we give praise and adorations to you Hapy."

We all stood up in the water and bowed our heads. "Amen-Ra," we all said together.

The high priest then looked into my eyes as he spoke, "Hold your breath." And he dunked me under the water for about five seconds, chanting a sacred prayer I could not quite understand. His parting words were, "Never allow the fears of others to become your fears. Never allow the limitations of others to become your limitations. Ride a higher wave. The wave of the Medjay is the way of Divine Spirit. Know that other possibilities exist for your life, Mentchu-hotep. I say this not as just the Hem Sem Tepy of this sacred temple, but as a fellow Medjay."

Medjay Bennu Henenu pushed our royal boat away from the dock as the singers, they kept singing until our boat was out of sight. Again Medjay Ni-Sobek and Medjay Bennu Henenu continued the rowing. I thought about the words of the Hem Sem Tepy, his great wisdom, and he was a Medjay. Wow! When we reached the temples of Ta Sna and Djeba, there were priests waiting for us, and we just passed them the packages almost without stopping, in perfect harmony like a baton pass in a relay race.

Once we reached Nebet, there were wab priests all along the causeway where the boats docked, dressed in all white with shiny bald heads. They all were engaged in some kind of washing detail, and they never even looked up at us. But in front of the twin temple of Nebet, there were several rows of priests involved in a sun-gazing ritual. I had seen the ritual done many times before but not at high noon, only in the morning and evening times. Medjay Bennu Henenu told me later that only full priests did sun gazing at high noon, and it was called absorbing Ra while riding the wings of Heru to higher consciousness. The Hem Ntchr Tepy of the temple greeted us with his assistant, and we exchanged bows and greetings just like we did at the great temple of Behdet. The Hem Ntchr Tepy asked Medjay Sia-en-hotep and Medjay Ka en Jhutyms to join them in their ritual. They were delighted after that long boat ride. I wanted to watch but Medjay Bennu Henenu signaled for me to follow them as Medjay Ni-Sobek secured our boat. We were to go to the market and pick up a few supplies for our stay at Abu. These priests wore two kinds of robes even though they were the same style, one half had on white-and-gold robes and the other half had white-and-red robes. The Heru side wore white and gold, and the Sobek side wore white-and-red robes. Wow, such beauty to see them all flowing in total harmony as if they were somehow connected physically. I was supposed to be helping the Medjay shop, but I never took my eyes off the priest. After standing in a very unusual posture for about fifteen minutes gazing at the Ra, they all began a very slow moving form of meditation, all sixty or so priests. Their sun gazing form consisted of one hundred moves or so. Once it was completed, they chanted something I could not understand and started the same slow moving form in the opposite direction, and it was as if it was one soul moving in harmony with the universe.

I looked at my two Medjay warriors and said, "Will we ever get to learn that?"

Medjay Ni-Sobek said, "In time, little brother. We all have much work to do, mentally, physically, and spiritually before we are in their league!" We all smiled, but I was thinking he was being kind, which was an understatement. *I'll be fifty before I could get to wash their clothes*, I thought.

Once we returned, the entire priestship had vanished inside, only the Hem Ntchr Tepy stood outside the temple walls with Medjay Sia- en-hotep and Medjay Ka-en-Jhutyms.

Again we greeted each other, the Hem Ntchr Tepy said, "Please do not rise, I am your humble servant and thank you for stopping at our twin temple Nebet before continuing on your journey to Abu. We have already placed limewater and fruit on your vessel. You will now come with us to the sacred feeding ritual of Sobek before you leave."

Once around the sacred pool, the priest held several fish in their hands as they chanted a hymn to Sobek the crocodile, Ntchr of the temple.

"Hail to you, Sobek, *anedj hr ek* Sobek," I jumped back quickly because out of the pool, three giant crocodiles leaped out of the water. The priest did not move, and the Medjay did not move. I was the only one who moved as I stood back from the pool as the huge crocodiles swam around the priest. Then altogether, the priest placed the fishes into the giant crocodiles' mouths. As the crocodiles swallowed the fish, there was a knowing, an exchange of energies, a feeling of balance between the priest and the Medjay and the crocodiles that words could not describe, a spiritual knowing. And once again, the priest sang their hymns to Sobek, and this was repeated several times before the ritual ended. We walked back to the boat without saying a word. Are they Medjay too? I had so many questions, it wasn't funny, but I held them all in.

Once we were all on our sacred royal Heru vessel, Medjay Sia-en- hotep advised us to eat the rest of the fruit before our journey to Abu. "Watch carefully how they are rowing the boat, young prince. These two Medjay warriors are master spear-and-staff fighters. This rowing is part of their training. They will teach you their training mythology because the long bo and spear are the first weapons you must master. I have been told that you have mastered the basics. That is good," said Medjay Sia-en-hotep. The next thing I knew, I was rowing and rowing and rowing. I think I rowed myself to sleep. I don't even remember going to bed. I only remembered blackness and rowing.

The next morning at Abu, I was excited. My arms and shoulders were a little sore, but it was a good sore. I had never rowed in that style before and never for that long. I did an early morning meditation, then stance training and swimming training. A few of these Medjay looked like they were breathing underwater, and later they showed me how one Medjay stayed underwater for three hours without coming up to the surface.

He used a thin, hollowed reed stem to breathe through. Each Medjay carried a reed tube in their belt.

Now I'm learning the tricks of the trade, the real secrets, I thought. That's how Medjay Jhutyms Ka-en-Heru could go underwater for ten minutes and wrestle that crocodile without coming up for air. Wow, I think he drowned the crocodile.

These Medjay at the camp ate no flesh, only fruits, vegetables, nuts, legumes, beans, and seeds. Everyone seemed to have unlimited energy. This was nothing like the junior training schools in Kemet that I had been in. They followed very strict eating habits when in training. They eat two main meals a day, but they could drink and eat fruits, nuts, and berries that were in seasons when needed but never ate late at night.

We had staff training early afternoon. Yes, now let's see if I can use the stuff I was taught. Medjay Bennu placed a special powered herb in some water for me, and it seemed to give me a special power kick. They reviewed my staff form, made corrections and then taught me three new staff attacks along with their defenses. *I love this stuff*, I thought. Everyone was so helpful, and I had to keep remembering I was the only one there that was not a Medjay. There were about two hundred Medjay warriors here, and I was definitely the youngest. I saw maybe four dozen young Medjay, maybe eighteen or nineteen years old, but they were all from Kash. And like Medjay Ka-en-Jhutyms, they were born doing this stuff.

During the next month, I saw very little of Medjay Sia-en-hotep or Medjay Ka-en-Jhutyms. They were busy teaching classes. But Medjay Ni-Sobek and Medjay Bennu Henenu were never out of my sight. They were two of the best staff and spear fighters I had ever seen. One afternoon, after staff-bo training, Medjay Bennu was giving me some pointers on the main difference between the bo staff and the spear when I asked him, "Is your staff fighting better than Ka-en-Jhutyms or Medjay Sia-en-hotep?"

He laughed. "No one here in this camp can beat them."

"You got to be joking," I said. "Your pole and spear fighting is impeccable."

"Compared to whose standards? You haven't really seen them fight, have you?" He smiled.

"I saw them at the homecoming against those Asian masters." "I could have beaten them," said Medjay Bennu Henenu.

"I saw Medjay Sia-en-hotep fight twenty warriors with swords when we were in Sparta, and all he had was a spear. He killed them all in about ten minutes. Then lead us into battle untouched."

"How about Medjay Ka-en-Jhutyms? He never speaks," I said. "Don't let that fool you, I saw them training one day on the boat

with high waves rocking the boat hard. Medjay Ka-en-Jhutyms never lost his balance, and he took the bo staff out of Medjay Sia-en-hotep's hands about three or four times with no effort. And they are not the best," said Medjay Bennu.

"I know, I have seen Medjay Jhutyms Ka-en-Heru," I said. "But he is not real. He is like the Ntchru."

"There are great spiritual teachers called the immortal Psdju or the nine immortals. They are Djedi. Chief Medjay

Jhutyms Ka-en-Heru is one of them, and the Shemsu Heru Tut-Ankh-Ra's elder brother is a Djedi also. The Djedi are the ultimate warrior-priests and warrior- priestesses, and they have been seen wearing hooded robes. And they carry some kind of crystal staff or wand of power," Medjay Bennu Henenu said.

"A true spiritual teacher helps to awaken your power by leading you back to your greatest you. By reminding you that you are a unique expression of Ntchr and have every right to be who you are and what your soul aspires to be. Such a teacher will never demand that you stand in awe of his/her light. Medjay Sia-en-hotep and Medjay Ka-en- Jhutyms, they will insist that you discover the light within you."

"Well, I'm glad of that. Medjay Ka-en-Jhutyms seem to defy all the laws of nature. Like his father, there is something about the twinkle in his eyes. Maybe they are from the star system Palladian," I said as we both laughed.

After our two months were up, Medjay Sia-en-hotep tested our staff pole and spear and was pleased. He fought both Medjay Bennu Henenu and Medjay Ni-Sobek at the same time, but both Medjay held their own. He snatched the pole out of my hand twice, but he also said he was pleased with my progress even though he beat me with his bare hands while I had the pole.

"Let's move on," he said. We rowed our royal Heru boat to the city of Dju em Hat in a section of Kash called Wawat. There we met Ta-Sety two-handed stick fighters, and for about a week, we exchanged ideas and fighting philosophies.

"There might be a time when your long pole is useless because of a lack of space or your pole breaks or is cut in half.

44

You must take advantage of every situation. Remember, a Medjay must prevail," said Medjay Sia-en-hotep.

I asked for permission to speak. "Yes, young Prince Mentchu-hotep," said Medjay Sia-en-hotep.

"Why didn't we spank them with our pole fighting? We were much better than them."

"Medjay Ni-Sobek, why didn't we spank them?" asked Medjay Sia-en-hotep.

"When training with outsiders, never let your opponent know all that you know. You might have to meet that same opponent on the battlefield."

"Thank you. We were there to learn their skills, not really to teach them ours."

"Now we will travel to the sacred city of Buhen, here we will sharpen our skills in the art of tool and weapon making. We will sharpen our arrows, spear tips, and swords. And last but not least, we will restring and refine our bows to prepare for the famous bowmen of Kerma."

On the upper left, two artisans prepare to place a caldron containing metal on a fire. The starter brick has been covered with a mound of charcoal pellets that has turned red with flames. Note the extra piles of charcoal at the ready and the large pottery vessels from which they have been emptied. Also note the two men stepping back and forth as they dance on padded feet upon a platform that appears to act as a kind of bellows. The glyph for /km/ black very likely based on the shape of these charcoal-fed fires and its meaning on the black carbon material that made the smelting process possible.

After five weeks of hard work, learning to smelt iron from ore and to forge our own weapons from the depths of our souls, I was really learning what being a Medjay was all about. For the first time, I was beginning to connect the dots on why the Shemsu Heru were invincible warriors. They were all blacksmiths and masters of metalwork. We created weapons that were extensions of our own bodies, minds, and souls. Each Medjay's weapon was part of his or her consciousness following the symmetry of our own molecular structure, using the golden ratio or golden spiral. I learn this sacred science back in the beloved temples in Waset. We were combining the spirit world and the physical world together by using the esoteric sciences for understanding the way of Ma'at.

The next day was a day of rest before moving on to Kerma. I spent most of the day in deep meditation. In my head, I was reviewing everything I learned like it was a Mdw Ntchr class. As I meditated on some of the Medjay training methods of combat, I realized that they were founded on the inner esoteric system of perceiving not only the world, but also the cosmos just like the Mdw Ntchr. Regular warriors approach combat by using everyday logic, speed, plus power with an excellent delivery equals success. This is exoteric learning. So when reading the walls of the sacred temples and text in Kemet, one can learn grammar and vocabulary and develop a general and sufficient exoteric meaning of the Mdw Ntchr. But to learn the esoteric meaning of the Medjay warriorship, one needs to think in the same way as those who created the Medjay system or the Mdw Ntchr text. Esoteric is not to be understood as a method of writing or combat but as the spirit of the practitioner, warrior, or writer of the Mdw Ntchr. It is that which cannot be clearly transcribed not from intent to hide, but because animal cerebral intelligence and also your reptilian brain really thinks this world is real and, therefore, are unfit to comprehend the infinite spirit.

So when the Hem Ntchr Tepy Dagi said to *initiate*, he actually means "to cause to begin" or "to cause to enter into." He was saying an initiate is one who has penetrated into the understanding and innerstanding of the vital matrix not just knowledge that results from the sensory observation of appearances, which the mind has created, but also we are learning the science of Divine Spirit. Now I remembered hearing the chief Medjay Jhutyms Ka-en-Heru say, "True teaching is not just an accumulation of knowledge. It is an awaking of consciousness, which goes through successive stages. The teachings of the way are called enlightenment because it reveals hidden energy, things that cannot be seen or even felt by normal humans. Practically, your entire mind is unconscious to you just like almost all of an iceberg is underneath the surface of the water, not visible to you."

I was on a roll, and to top it off, that night Medjay Ka-en-Jhutyms taught a profound class on astronomy that just blew me away. The night sky will never ever look the same to me again. Understanding the stars is a language. If you understand this language, the night sky speaks to you. But at least now I know where the star system Pleiadian is. I thought she made that up. This star system is a small cluster of seven visible stars located in Heru's vision of Haap, the great bull, which is close to five hundred light years from the planet Earth. The Pleiadians are a very ancient race of humanoids. They have traveled to Earth in ancient times and are an advanced, peaceful race.

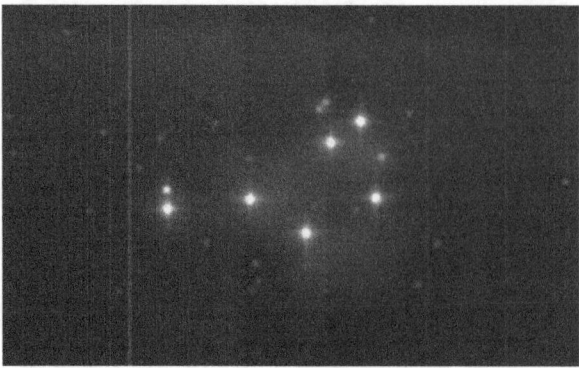

The Pleiadian star system

Medjay Ka-en-Jhutyms said that reality is invisible and anything that can be perceived or observed in any way, even measured scientifically, is an illusion. This is the opposite of what the world thinks, and even most of the people I know think who are not Medjay or spiritual priests. If nothing is outside of your mind, then to judge it is to grant it power over you and to not judge it is to withdraw its power over you. I will have to work on that skill.

Medjay Ka-en-Jhutyms also said in the same discussion that 95 percent of the so-called universe is dark, triple blackness, or hidden from you. Not only is it correlating to the unconscious mind, but also its set up that way so you can continue to make discoveries about it and look for answers in the universe instead of in your conscious mind where all the answers really are. The so-called history or even ourstory of the universe—past, present, and future—is simply a script that was written by the ego.

I remember Chief Medjay Jhutyms Ka-en-Heru saying something to me when I asked him where we were and how he knew we were there if he had never been there before. He was extremely patient with me, and he never lost his temper in two and half years.

With a smile on his face, he said, "Really, you are nowhere because all that you see is an illusion. So if nothing exists, you can't be lost because you are really not here. But if we choose to participate in this dream, seek not to change the world, but choose to change your mind about the world. Listen carefully, the earth has a magnetic force field or grid around it as it is connected to Ra. Just like our illusionary bodies have a force field around it and is connected to Geb, the earth, and that our pineal gland is linked to this grid. With our inner vision produced by the pineal gland, we can see a illusion of the earth with us in it so we always know where we are on the planet just like a falcon or a vulture who may travel hundreds of miles in a day, but they are never lost.

"So astrology is the study of the planets and heavenly bodies as it relates to human beings on this imaginary grid, using Heru's vision." The chief Medjay also said, "The body is not what it seems to be with the naked eye. It is not a solid mass. It is actually a system of little particles or points of energy separated from each other by space and held in place through an electrically balanced field. When these particles are not in their proper place, then disease manifests in that body. Spiritual healing is one way of bringing the particles back in harmonious relationship. Healing requires a shift in perception. What appears to be sickness is all in the mind and has nothing to do with the body. So all healing is really done in the mind. All healing is spiritual, not physical." My head was spinning all night around Heru's vision.

Early the next morning, we were off to the sacred city of Kerma in the land of Kash.

"Young prince, I hear you are good with a bow and arrow. This part of Kash is called Ta-Sety, the land of the bow. You will see many wondrous things. Remember you are here to observe and learn, not to show off your skills. I want you to know even though you will see masters that can defy the laws of the Ntchru, no one in this town has greater skills than the Medjay spiritual priest and my and your young great master, Medjay Ka-en-Jhutyms," said Medjay Sia-en-hotep.

I was shocked again, and I thought Medjay Sia-en-hotep was in charge and was the senior Medjay on this mission especially since he was a member of Chief Medjay Jhutyms Ka-en-Heru's elite forces. But he cleared the air and let it be known that even though he was older and had trained longer, he was the student of Medjay Ka-en-Jhutyms who was a Medjay spiritual priest. And only through the will of Amen-Ra and Mentchu had he been honored with half his skills in his lifetime and, through Medjay Ka-en-Jhutyms permission, was allowed to be his voice. Every day I'm learning something different, and I have already learned more at fifteen inundations of Hapy under the rule of Shemsu Heru Nswt Intef-sa-Ra, most men will learn in two lifetimes. Amen-Ra is great, Dwa Ntchr!

I had read about Kerma from the works of Harkhuf the overseer of foreign countries of the south under Shemsu Heru Mery-en-Ra and Shemsu Heru Pepy Nefer-ka-Ra. In Kerma, the chief of the bow people and his royal court met us at the dock, and he, the chief of the bow people, escorted us into his village with a royal reception. There was dancing and drumming with beautiful and exotic women everywhere we looked. They tried to feed us wine and meat, but we only ate fruit because even the vegetables were cooked in meat. The Medjay were very alert even though this was a friendly mission. Kerma had fought against Kemet in several wars. Medjay Sia-en-hotep had warnedus that this could get ugly at anytime so be alert. Even during the night, they tried to send women to our sleeping quarters, but we turned them away. The next morning, there was a bow marksmanship demonstration in our honor. We saw some amazing marksmanship. They had ten archers hit ten bull's-eyes with arrows from fifty meters out. One bowman shot one target three times in the air before it could hit the ground. One bowman, while riding on a horse and doing all kinds of tricks, hit five bull's-eyes upside down, and it was like he couldn't miss. Afterward, we trained together and had target practice ourselves. I was fair, but the Medjay were just as good as the very best of the Ta-Sety bowmen. Medjay Sia-en-hotep threw two daggers at a tree maybe thirty meters away, and Medjay Ka-en-Jhutyms shot his bow and arrow blindfolded after him twice. When we looked closely at the tree, one arrow landed in the bull's-eye with one dagger, but the second arrow hit the very spot the daggers would enter before the dagger got there, which means Medjay Ka-en-Jhutyms knew the very spot the dagger would enter before the dagger itself knew. Now that was scary.

The chief was a little disturbed and jealous, so he asked for a challenge, one on one. Medjay Sia-en-hotep stepped forward, and then the chief's son steps out from behind a curtain with one of the most magnificent bows I have ever seen. His headdress was full of royal feathers, his muscles flexed and sparkled in the sun's rays, he stood maybe six feet six tall, and he spoke with power.

"We shall have a duel. Each man will have five arrows, and we will fight until only one man is standing." He took a deep breath. "We shall start at fifty meters." Medjay Ka-en-Jhutyms stopped Medjay Sia-en- hotep and signaled him to step back with the wave of his hand.

"I shall handle this," he said firmly. Everyone looked on with intense eyes. This was surely the high point of the day! What had just happened earlier with the bow and arrows and daggers shot past almost everybody's head, and only a few will get it the next morning.

The two warriors stood fifty meters away, the Medjay warrior versus the Ta-Sety bowman.

The chief said, "Are you ready, warriors?"

They nodded. "Then begin!"

The Ta-Sety bowman shot two quick arrows at Medjay Ka-en- Jhutyms who just blocked the first and caught the second arrow with is bare hand in thin air with a smile on his face. The whole crowd was in shock, even the chief of the Ta-Sety bowmen. The Medjay warrior started to run toward the bowman, zigzagging as he ran. The bowman shot the third and fourth arrows all on target, and the Medjay snatched them all out of the air. Then with a twirling zigzag move, he leaped into the air. The bowman shot his last arrow at the Medjay who was now about ten meters away, flying through the air. The Medjay caught the arrow with his teeth upside down. Then while twisting and twirling in the air, he landed with both his feet, kicking the bowman's face, knocking him to the ground, and landing on top of the bowman with one knee in his throat and the other foot on his chest, pinning him helplessly to the ground. Medjay Ka-en-Jhutyms looked up at the Ta- Sety bowman's chief who looked on in total shock and amazement at the powers of this Medjay warrior. And with one swift blow to the temple, the chief bowman's son lay helplessly unconscious. It was crystal clear to everyone there that the Medjay Ka-en-Jhutyms could have taken the chief's son's life at any time.

The Medjay Ka-en-Jhutyms took the arrow out of his mouth walked over to the chief and broke the arrow in half right in his face and said, "We came here in peace. Do not provoke us for we are Medjay, the greatest warriors on earth and heaven."

Their chief knelt down on one knee and bowed his head with respect, then he spoke, "Thank you for my son's life. I am forever in your debt."

As we climbed back into our royal Heru boat, it was quiet. No one said a word. No bowman from Ta-Sety came to see us off or accompanied us. Once we all were safely in the royal Heru boat, there was a long moment of silence, and then we all held each other's hand, right hand up, left hand down with our eyes close.

Medjay Sia-en-hotep spoke first, "What you have witnessed here the last few days is a lesson to remember. Everyone who smiles in your face is not your friend, and no matter how monstrous your enemy behaves, always have Ma'at in your heart. Even in the most joyous occasion, *esfet* is always standing by, ready to seize an opportunity to destroy you. We will see them again in battle. Remember their faces, but for the moment Amen-Ra, Ptah, Khnum, and Mentchu, which are all part of the one, are satisfied."

Medjay Ka-en-Jhutyms spoke, "The Medjay are training you through meditation on how to focus the mind on the Divine Spirit, not the illusionary world. When you are thinking with the ego like the Ta-Sety bowmen, that's wrong-mindedness, which is trapped in the dream. The verses when you are thinking with the Divine Spirit, that's right-mindedness and invincibility." He paused for a minute so we could digest what he said.

Then he continued, "There is no challenge to a Medjay spiritual priest of the Ntchr. Challenge implies doubt, and the trust on which the Medjay who is one with Ntchr teaches doubt is an illusion, therefore, it is nonexisting, making doubt impossible. You will come to know and experience that the Ntchr is not outside of you. When that happens, my fellow Medjay, you will no longer identify yourself with a vulnerable body or anything else that can be limited. You will learn instead of your true reality as pure spirit that is invulnerable forever."

We had about a three- or four-hour ride to our next destination, Napata. I was anxious to row, knowing this was going to improve my bow skills. I attacked the waters of Hapy with a whole new attitude, realizing what an honor to see such beauty and to be apart of an invincible Medjay team of spiritual warriors. As I stroked the magical waters of Hapy Eteru, my soul began to fill and tears clouded my eyes. Surely, I had been favored by Amen-Ra to be protected and trained by the kindest, gentlest, and yet most feared of all warriors on earth and in heaven.

CHAPTER 3

THE PRINCESS TEM

By late afternoon, our streamlined royal Heru boat, approached the ancient city of Napata. The scenery changed quickly from desert to lush green fields, to large plots of cultivated farmlands, and finally, to huge temples, castles, and monuments and the large wall in the city of Napata. I was here only three years ago, but now I was looking at Kash with a whole new set of eyes. My consciousness had expanded, and therefore, everything was different. Most people think that the Kemetyu of Kemet influenced Kash, but that's because they were never here. Kash was thousands of years older than Kemet. The deeper I traveled up south, the more obvious it became that this magnificent culture that we shared along the Hapy Valley originated here and flowed down north into Kemet, not the other way around. And the north and northeast all the way to Asia are our children when it comes to sacred knowledge and deep thought.

Military men at the port where we docked our boat immediately recognized our royal Heru boat and us as Medjay. One of them approached us. He knelt on one knee and bowed his head with one hand inside the other.

"May I escort you into the city?" he asked with great pride as he bowed his head.

Medjay Sia-en-hotep replied, "*Tiw*, yes, we are on official business of the royal court." I secured the ores while Medjay Bennu Henenu and Medjay Ni-Sobek leaped out of the boat quickly to secure it at the port.

"Wow!" yelled two little round-faced Napata boys.

One spoke, "Did you see how high and far they jumped? No one can do that. They must be Medjay. Look at that sword and bow— yes, they are Medjay." With excitement all around their little round brown faces, they vanished into the city. We always walked in the same formation: Medjay Sia-en-hotep walked in front, diagonal off his left shoulder and one step back was Medjay Ka-en-Jhutyms, diagonal to the right and one step back in the center was where I walked, diagonal to the left and one step back was Medjay Bennu Henenu, and diagonal to the right and one step back was Medjay Ni-Sobek at the rear. As we approached the city walls, it was very noisy and busy with common market people and farmers trading and haggling over items, but all eyes were on us as we passed.

The Medjay warriors were legendary in these lands. There wasn't a man, woman, or child who did not know of the awesome powers of the Medjay warriors, the greatest warriors on earth and heaven. The soldiers took us past customs and spoke for us, and within a few minutes, we were inside the sacred city of Napata. A carriage man tried to offer us a ride, but Medjay Sia-en-hotep waved him away. I also noticed that I was the only one of us smiling and looking all around like a tourist. There must be some unspoken rule that Medjay don't smile in public as they all had that same look. I wondered if they practiced this. I thought, *I better get it together. We are visiting the mayor of the city.*

As we stood in front of the royal palace dedicated to Het Heru in Napata, Medjay Ka-en-Jhutyms spoke to us, "The way of the Medjay teaches wisdom. Wisdom is dynamic motion, deep thought, and *nefer* speech in action. The power of dynamic motion can only be mastered after unlimited and relentless perfect repetition. The mastery or *Neb* of motion can stop the world, clearing the thoughts so that the infinite knowledge of the ancestors may guide your speech. Good speech, *Mdw Nefer*, is the light of wisdom. The light of wisdom is the lamp that lights the way to all knowledge. So, Medjay, when we speak, remember the words of my father, the chief Medjay Jhutyms Ka-en-Heru, that when the mouth stumbles in darkness, it is much worse than the foot. The Ntchr Jhuty is satisfied." We all stepped forward with our left leg and chanted, "Amen-Ra,

Dwa Ntchr, anedj *her rack Jhuty*, Anuk Jhuty, Jhuty," as we crossed our arms in front of our chest.

Medjay Ni-Sobek entered the palace first to prepare our way. I noticed the Mdw Ntchr writings on the walls were a little different, but the friezes on the walls were basically the same as in Kemet. Giant granite statues of the Holy Trinity— Asr, Ast, and Heru—stood in the center square alongside two long Tekhenwy. I could recognize all the Ntchru. I had become a budding scribe in Kemet amongst our own royal court at Waset. Legend has it that Asr was a real king from Kash thousands of years ago, and he was so great they deified him just like Imhotep was a real scribe, counselor, healer, astronomer, vizier, and architect of Shemsu Heru Netchrikhet during the first golden age in Kemet after the last great flood. And in some cities in Kemet, he is deified like the Ntchru as the Ntchr of health and medicine. I observed two sacred cobras on the forehead of the Kashite rulers, distinguishing them from Kemet rulers who wore only one cobra. And during the first golden age up until Shemsu Heru Nswt Bety Peppy, we wore a cobra and a vulture, representing Upper and Lower Kemet. We called it the Nebty, the two ladies. Nekhbet was the vulture from the south, and Wadjet was the cobra from the north. I also noticed that the Kashite rulers wore a gold thumb ring. The great thumb ring was used for pulling a bowstring, recalling the fame of the Kashite archers. I smiled as I looked down on my thumb ring, my chest swelled with pride because all the Medjay warriors wore them.

Medjay Ni-Sobek returned with several members of the royal court. I was pleasantly surprised. The mayor was a young man, maybe twenty- three years old or so. He introduced himself as Prince Piye, son of Shemsu Heru Tut-Ankh-Ra of Napata. I also noticed the very colorful clothing of the members of the royal court, and they wore fewer clothes here than in our Kemet temples.

The temperature was much hotter here during the day, maybe 120 degrees Fahrenheit. Medjay Sia-en-hotep then introduced our team, leaving me for last.

"Prince, meet prince." Prince Piye smiled, and we all chuckled. "This is the crown prince Mentchu-hotep from Waset, eldest son of Shemsu Heru Nswt Intef-sa-Ra."

We greeted each other with great affection and respect. Two royal servants dressed with class and matching outfits came with tea for us as we sat in a spacious library filled with papyrus scrolls. The library had huge colorful columns like back in Kemet. Prince Piye said he was envious of me, a young prince who was a Medjay warrior. I explained that I was not a Medjay yet but studying to be an initiate. He mentioned that his elder brother, Crown Prince Ipi, was the Medjay in his family. "So while my brother learned to fight and travel the world, I was locked in the library with thousands of papyrus scrolls, but I love to fight too."

We laughed a lot as he asked me many questions about the state of Kemet and my royal family. Medjay Ni-Sobek and Medjay Bennu Henenu left to buy supplies for our three-day journey up the Hapy Eteru. If the waters and the rain would allow, we would be at the mouth of where the blue and white Hapy met in three days' journey. Medjay Sia-en-hotep and Medjay Ka-en-Jhutyms stood patiently by while Prince Piye and I talked about how different but yet how similar our two worlds were, and we pledged to maintain this new friendship and communication.

The prince introduced me to his two sisters, the princesses. I was stunned for a moment as one of the princesses was the young girl I met back at Waset, the girl who totally blew me away and told me I must be from the star system Pleiadian.

"Prince Mentchu-hotep, meet Princess Kawit and Princess Tem."

Princess Tem smiled, holding a blue lotus flower to her face while bowing her head, and I bowed back with a smile on my face also. The little one, Princess Kawit, just giggled, hiding behind her big sister's long dress. The prince looked surprised.

"Do you know Princess Tem?"

"No, but I have seen her in Waset at the royal temple of Ipet Asut." "Yes, she studied there for several years. She is a full priestess of Het Heru, in fact, she studied under your royal mother, Hmt Nswt wrt Iah. And this royal princess really ruins this temple. She is unbelievably efficient, I'm just the figurehead." We all laughed.

"The princess Tem can show you around the palace, Prince Mentchu- hotep. She knows every little detail, and take your time. While Medjay Sia en-hotep and my second most famous Medjay next to his father Chief Medjay Jhutyms Ka-en-Heru, my teacher Medjay Ka-en-Jhutyms talk business, he might even show me a trick or two if I beg him. I have to be ready for my cocky big brother, crown prince Medjay Ipi." We all smile as we parted ways.

Princess Tem spoke my language quite elegantly as well as several others, and I was very impressed again for the second time. She was younger than I but much more mature and definitely much wiser. She was already running a temple and handling trade and international affairs, and I was not even a Medjay initiate yet.

"You are so young, and you are running a sacred temple and especially one as important as the temple of Het Heru," I said.

She just smiled and said, "Your mother was a Hemet Sem Tepy when she was my age." She replied in perfect Mdw Ntchr.

"I bet you know my mother better than I," the young prince replied. The young princess Tem rang a bell, and two priestesses arrived within a few seconds.

"Please take Princess Kawit to her room and twist her hair for me."

The two priestesses bowed their heads.

"Tiw, Hmt Sem Tepy Tem," they both spoke together in harmony. Princess Kawit seemed a little disturbed, but she did not complain as she followed the two priestesses down the hallway and out of sight.

The princess continued, "Your mother is so proud of you. She talks about you all the time, and so does your little sister, Royal Princess Neferu. I'm only two years older than her and two years younger than you, Crown Prince Mentchu-hotep. You gave your little sister Neferu and your mother a diamond necklace wrapped in gold in the shape of an ankh from Ta Ntchr, and your little sister, Neferu, says she will never take it off. She sleeps with it and bathes with it on. She says as long as she wears it, you will always be close to her heart, and her love for you will protect you and keep you safe. Neferu said the law of love provides limitless power and possibilities for those who are in attunement with it." "I never knew that," I said in surprise. She took me by my hand as we walked through a large hypostyle hallway with giant decorated columns dedicated to Het Heru.

"I promised your mother and Neferu I would take good care of you." We just stood quietly for a long while, then she read the Mdw Ntchr off the walls, and I thought my Mdw Ntchr was *nefer*.

"I praise the golden Ntchrt, I exalt her majesty, I raise high the lady of heaven, I make praise for Het Heru and chant for my mistress."

"Your mother Hemet Nswt Wrt-Hmt Ntchr Tepy en Het Heru Iah said I would be the perfect Hmt for you," she said while smiling.

"My mother said that?" I said with a surprised look on my face. "But then again, my mother always had impeccable taste."

We both laughed out loud hysterically. *Good thing no one else was around*, we both thought.

"Over there is the sacred reading room in the library where my brother, Prince Piye, spends most of his time. He has read almost every papyrus here. Some are more than four thousand years old."

"He is quite impressive," I said to Princess Tem.

"We are all very proud of him especially his big brother Medjay Ipi," she said. "Now this room is the Holy of Holies. Only my father, my two brothers, and I can enter this sacred space." Her voice changed along with her whole attitude.

"I bring a sacred offering of food and flowers to my mother, Het Heru, twice a day, and I sing songs to praise her in all her glory." She opened up the shrine's door, and one of the most beautiful statues of Het Heru that I have ever seen was glittering gold in the soft candlelight. It stood about two feet tall in absolute perfect symmetry. I just stood in the doorway, mesmerized as she held it in her delicate hands. Then she began to sing, and she blew me away again for the third time. She was a gorgeous, magnificent princess, high priestess of Het Heru, with a voice of Ma'at. And I just stood there speechless. When she finished her song, she kissed the golden statue of Het Heru and then placed it back in its magnificent miniature shrine case gilded in gold, and then she closed the inner shrine door. She then picked up a small broom and cleared her footsteps as she walked backward out of the shrine space of the Holy of Holies and locked the outer door behind her.

"*Nefer aa, Nefer aa*, that was magnificent," I said to her. "I've only heard my mother sing like that."

Princess Tem took me by the hand again and said, "Then you haven't heard your little sister, Princess Neferu, sing? She has the voice of Ma'at. Well, your mother taught your little sister and me that song, and she is my teacher. And since my real mother is in heaven, I'm claiming your mother as my earthly mother too. You know your grandfather and your father's brothers are my grandfather and father's teachers. And yes, this temple looks very much like your magical Kemet, but I've managed to give it a very Kashite Napata twist." We both fell out laughing again. "Come meet Priest Kha-f-Ptah. He is our chief architect and engineer, and he comes from a long line of architects, twenty-three generations of priests, astronomers, and architects."

As we walked into his chambers, he stood up gracefully. His posture was very strong, and I could feel his power as I gazed at him eye to eye. We stood about the same height, but his face was very dark with the light of wisdom.

"Ye m hotep Hem Ntchr Kha-f-Ptah." I bowed my head with my right hand inside the left to him.

Princess Tem spoke, "His great-grandfather rebuilt this temple in honor of your great-grandmother who was a great Medjay priestess- warrior, Hmt Nswt Wrt Neferu of Napata." Priest Kha-f-Ptah smiled.

"She's our ourstorian around here, and she's quite impressive." "Stop," she said, "don't embarrass me." He smiled very modestly.

I asked, "What is that symbol on both of your shoulders? I have never seen that before."

"My family is from Meroe, and this is the Naforb'a, it is a very ancient Kash symbol that represents the five primary forces of Natoru (the nature of all nature, the highest Ntchr-Ntchrt, Ntchru). The Naforb'a can be found throughout various ancient cultures across the world where the Shemsu Heru of ancient Kash have traveled as a symbol of well-being, peace, tranquility, and harmony. The very word *Naforb'a* means 'good soul' because when you live in harmony with these five primary forces, you will experience nothing but peace and tranquility. In your Kemet society, it has been replaced with Ma'at. They are one and the same."

"Dwa Ntchr for your clarity and foresight," I said.

"*Nn, hapana,* no, the pleasure was all mine, young crown prince Mentchu-hotep. For the Kashite people of Meroe, every person is an incarnation, a spirit who has taken on a body. So our true nature is spiritual. The world is where one comes to carry out specific projects. A birth is therefore the arrival of someone, usually an ancestor that somebody already knows, which has an important task to do here. May your ancestors continue to guide you. I see your great-grandfather in you. May you continue to listen. I see Naforb'a in you."

He bowed his head and placed his hands together as he excused himself.

"Wow, he seemed to be extremely deep minded, I would love to sit at his feet and absorb his knowledge and wisdom."

"I assure you, Crown Prince Mentchu-hotep, your paths will meet again many times."

"You say that with great confidence." She just smiled. I was like melted butter in her hands. Her wish was my command, and for the moment, Princess Tem was all I could think about.

"Your necklace, how beautiful. I recognize these stones—amethyst, garnet, opal, lapis lazuli, and onyx. You must be born under the Heru sign of Hapy. You represent the element of air, but you are the water bearer, the priest, or in your case, the priestess that pours the libation for the blessings of good fortune and prosperity in the house of enlightenment. And to top all that beauty off, you're wearing your favorite colors, indigo and purple."

The princess smiled. "So I see your mother has taught you well." She smiled again.

"And I know that you were born under that same glorious Heru sign also." We both laughed.

"You know, I'm really beginning to like you, Priestess Tem."

"The feeling is neutral, but I liked you the very first time I saw you," she said. I was speechless again.

The next day everyone was busy preparing for our trip, everyone except me. My mind was only on Princess Tem.

Medjay Sia-en-hotep put his magical left hand around my left shoulder and spoke softly. "We will be leaving in the morning, you should say good-bye to the prince and princess for us. You think you could do that? Communication is important," he said.

"*Tiw*, it would be an honor, Medjay Sia-en-hotep."

"Good, Medjay Bennu Henenu and Medjay Ni-Sobek will escort you to the palace after dinner."

After dinner, I asked Medjay Ka-en-Jhuty if he could explain something for me.

"If all of this is an illusion and we are not our bodies, then do we really have a soul?"

Ka-en-Jhuty smiled. "I appreciate your question, young Prince Mentchu-hotep, and the answer is *tiw hena nen*! You don't have a soul. You are a soul, and you have a body. Even within the illusion, the imaginary body has purpose and a mission so the soul that is an aspect of the spirit can return home, a state of oneness with the Divine Spirit in heaven. What is important here is your attitude while you're in this illusion on your mission. *Tiw*, I am a living soul. My body is a perfect instrument of my indwelling soul. *Tiw*, I dwell within this wonderful, magnificent body—temple for which I am grateful as an impeccable spiritual warrior. And because I am clear about my purpose while I'm on my mission, I intend for this soul to expose its light and love through me to all with whom I come in contact and who are in my illusionary world."

"Wow, I have a lot to learn, great Neb, and how about women and understanding sexuality?"

"Sexual identity, as we know it, exists only in this illusionary human life form. It is not of the soul or the Divine Spirit. These types of divine questions must be directed to my father. You are on your own concerning these matters. Just remember Ma'at, and you will be fine." During the heat of the early afternoon, Princess Tem like most Napatians, bathed several times a day in an attempt to stay clean and to keep the heat at bay. She thought about the young crown prince, Mentchu-hotep, how strong and handsome he was. She smiled to herself on his mastery of gemstones and colors. Hemet Nswt Wrt Iah had taught all her students the art of color therapy. Much of Kemet and Kash's *Saa* (spiritual protection) were made with colorful gemstones because of the pure colors they reflected. She looked at her favorite *Saa*, which was supposed to protect her and correct disharmony in her body.

The crown prince and she shared the same colors and gemstones.

Would Princess Neferu share and allow him to love another woman? she thought. She had even entertained the idea in her head even before she knew how wonderful he was. As she stroked her long, beautiful dark-brown legs in her private pool, she thought how nice it would be to share a bath with Prince Mentchu-hotep. She could rub away all his stress from his tired muscles after his training. She was a master at massage healing and pressure points, and she could be his second heaven, she thought.

"Thank you for seeing me this evening, Princess Tem. We will be traveling to Meroe tomorrow morning, and on behalf of our royal Medjay team, we thank you and your brother, the mayor, Prince Piye, for your royal hospitality."

"*Dua Ntchr*, great minds think alike. I had already arranged for our musicians and dancers to perform for you tonight. I was on my way to get you when you arrived."

"Dua Ntchr," I mumbled in a low voice to myself.

Princess Tem smiled. "I hope it stops raining, the Hapy Eteru is very dangerous this time of the year," she replied.

Napata was a great metropolis. Most of its buildings were made of hard stone, and there were sections in the older part of the city made of red bricks.

"How old is this city?" I asked Princess Tem. She smiled. "And was that a real castle I saw yesterday near the front wall?" I asked.

"Of course it is, it's a military warehouse," she replied. "We have been building castles like the one you saw for more than three thousand years." "The Amen priest told me that the city of Napata was two thousand years old when the priest Narmer united Upper and Lower Kemet into one nation-state, Sema Tawy."

"Look outside across the walkway," she pointed. "Over there, that statue of Ptah standing twenty-five meters tall is made of solid diorite rock just like the statue of Kha-f-Ra at the foot of Heru em Akhety in Lower Kemet. This statue of Ptah was erected also around the time of the high priest Narmer."

"That's incredible, and what an exquisite finish. Ptah was the greatest of Kemet Ntchru during the time of Shemsu Heru Narmer."

"*Tiw*, I know, he was Neb of truth, ruler of the sky, and master of both worlds and patron Ntchr to all the craftsmen, the creative spark of light in every human soul," she said.

I smiled. "You have been taught well, and you are brilliant."

"So are you, Crown Prince Mentchu-hotep, maybe you're not from Pleiadian after all." We laughed hysterically together.

This feels so right, walking next to him, she thought. "If it feels right, it's right. If it doesn't feel right, it's not right." These were the words of her spiritual mother, Hmt Nswt Wrt Iah.

Then she would say, "Ask yourself these questions: Is what you feel Ma'at? Do you trust yourself to do Ma'at? Because at the end of the day, Ma'at is the foundation of everything great and good. You need it to communicate with the spirit world, but you also need it in all areas of life. You can't be a great diviner without Ma'at, nor a great healer or a great artist or a great leader or a great priestess or a great friend or even a great lover. But you cannot buy Ma'at at the market. It must come from within. You have to work at it and own it. The best way to cultivate Ma'at is to start practicing it every day."

Mentchu-hotep stopped for a moment. Just like Priestess Tem who was in deep thought, so was he.

He looked in her eyes and said, "I have never been to the sacred cities to the north of Lower Kemet. I have not seen the great Mer Khut of Khufu, Men-Ka-Ra, and Kha-f-Ra. I long to touch the paws of Heru-m-Akhety and to kneel and pray before the Mer Khut of Snefru, Nswt Bety Huni, and Heru Netchrikhet. Princess Tem, when I turn my nightly dreams into a reality of my daytime dream, I will be the Nswt Bety, Shemsu Heru Mentchu-hotep."

He said this like he already had the title, she thought.

"I believe you, and I hope I am part of your life when that happens." She smiled.

He gently touched both her hands as he looked into her liquid eyes. "Thank you, that was very kind of you."

"It was from my heart," she said.

"I know, I can see you." He held her in his arms with a warm embrace for several seconds.

"Thank you for gently bringing me into the light. I see you too. When someone truly sees you and, in caring, urges you into the warmth of a loving embrace, you leave the darkness in which you have taken refuge and come once more into the light of love."

Now she really had my head spinning in circles, I thought. I tried to clear my head as we walked toward her sacred palace along the wide streets of Napata. I had forgotten all about the rain or Medjay Bennu and Ni-Sobek who walked behind us. Along the way, I could see all the crafts I saw in Waset: blacksmiths, goldsmiths and coppersmiths, carpenters and cabinetmakers, weavers, potters, glass blowers, shoemakers, masons, and tailors.

"Your dress looks wonderful on you, Princess Tem."

"Dwa Ntchr," she replied, "this is Napatian cotton mixed with Asian silk, some of the finest in the world!"

"I see, you have impeccable taste like my mother."

"*Tiw,* your mother is my teacher." She smiled. When we arrived at the royal palace, the musicians, dancers, and singers were all in place and ready. I was amazed at all the different instruments: horns, guitars, flutes, triangles, pipes, trumpets, harps, and drums, several types of drums.

We sat in a small theatre with unbelievable artwork all around us. The room had rounded corners made specially to amplify the sound. She waved her hand, and the music started like a smooth wave on a sandy beach.

"I'll let you in on one of our royal secrets," Princess Tem whispered into the crown prince's ear.

"Music is magical. We use sacred music like this with the harp in the shape of the golden spiral to stimulate plant growth and increase crop yields."

"Are you serious?" I said. She smiled at me.

"Look at the growth of these plants, very serious, can you feel it all the way down to your soul?"

Wait till I return home to Waset, I thought. *Divine music therapy as a tool for healing the people in our family and the royal court. Divine harp music for our indoor gardens and for improving the village crops. Tiw,* the plants looked well loved. Then he thought of something the chief Medjay told him in reference to how he knew so much about plants and nature and what herb to use.

"Anything will give up its secrets if you love it enough."

Kash is unbelievable, he thought. After the smooth, soothing music, the tempo changed, and the dancers came on to their beautifully designed and well-lit stage.

"They are really good," I said after several minutes of watching their magical steps.

I whispered to Princess Tem. "I even recognized a few of the dancers from the sacred temple of Amen-Ra. Those two dancers I've seen in the Temple at Waset." I pointed at them with excitement to Princess Tem, and then she giggled.

"So you're the cute quiet little student they told me about?"

"What?"

CHAPTER 4

HAPY ETERU

Hapy Eteru, the longest river in the world

Finally, we were off to the legendary city of Khartoum. This is the place where the two magical waters of the blue and white

Hapy Eteru meet. I had dreamed about traveling to the sources of the Hapy Eteru, the longest river in the world, over 4,160 miles or 6,825 kilometers long. We learned about these magical places in the sacred temples of Kemet, but to experience Hapy is another world in itself. I've spent my whole life traveling up and down Hapy. I could even hear the voice of my father, the Shemsu Heru Intef, telling me that Hapy was the artery of life and blood for the entire Kemet civilization. Now I was realizing that I really didn't know the Ntchr Hapy. I have only been introduced to a small portion of its tremendous depth. I knew that Hapy Resewt was Hapy of the south and wore the cluster of lotus plants on its head. Hapy Meht, Hapy of the north, wore the cluster of papyrus on its head. I knew that Hapy Eteru supplied Kemet with 98 percent of its water. I had even memorized a sacred hymn to Hapy from the Mer Khut shabyt, the pyramid text, from Shemsu Heru Huni's sacred shrine.

Adoration of Hapy

Hail to you Hapy, sprung from earth, come to nourish Kemet. Of secret ways to whom his followers sing.

Who floods the fields that Ra has made? To nourish all who thirst.

Let's drink the waterless desert. His dew descending from the sky.

Food provider, bounty maker, who creates all that is good. Neb of awe, sweetly fragrant, gracious when he comes. Who makes herbage for the herbs, gives sacrifice for every Ntchru. Dwellings in the Duat, he controls both sky and earth.

Mfundishi Jhutyms Ka en Heru Hassan Kamau Salim

Conqueror of the two lands.

He fills the stores, makes bulge the barns, and gives bounty to the poor. Dua Ntchr Hapy.

For the next three days into our journey, it rained extremely hard as we rowed up the Hapy Eteru. Even in the rain, the scenery was breathtaking, dangerous but breath taking. The Hapy banks had flooded, and we could not even see the river's edge. We were caught into a heavy downpour of floodwaters that rushed in from the Atbara River at speeds more than fifty miles an hour. We were heading for one of the cataracts at a speed of more than sixty miles per hour. Our royal Heru boat was out of control, and we lost both our oars when the royal

Heru boat was thrown upside-down with us in it. It was a miracle we were still alive. Only the long swimming exercises and emergency drills that we endured at the Medjay training camp back in Abu allowed us to hold on to our boat while it was still underwater for maybe two minutes or so. When we surfaced, we could see the large rocks on the right side and a thirty-foot drop onto a pile of jagged rocks to our left. Either side, it was sudden death in about forty-five seconds. Our options were to drown, be smashed, be crushed or ripped apart, or maybe even be eaten by Hapy crocodiles swimming around also out of control. These seemed to be the choices we had. The current was too strong to swim, and we only had time to pray. I was just going to close my eyes and beg Amen-Ra and my grandfather, Shemsu Heru Mentchu-hotep, for forgiveness for not completing my mission.

I heard Medjay Ka-en-Jhutyms say, "Give me the rope and hold on." By this time, we had about ten seconds left, and I could see the mist from the thirty-foot drop. I just started counting.

"Sfku, sisu, diu, fdu, shmut, snu, wa, ahhhhhhh!" I screamed at the top of my voice as the royal Heru boat stopped with a huge jolt at the edge of the cliff. I looked up, and water was splashing everywhere. We were still alive, and I was choking from swallowing so much water. Medjay Ka-en-Jhutyms had tied the rope around his waist and was swimming against the current to the shore. The only thing holding me in the boat was Medjay Sia-en-hotep, and he had one arm around me and the other holding on to the boat while Medjay Ni-Sobek. And Medjay Bennu Henenu were both holding on to the rope and the boat. We were still in danger of being pulled by the mighty current, but Medjay Ka-en-Jhutyms just kept stroking away like a shark cutting through the current, pulling the royal Heru boat all the way to the shore. The rest of us were so weak, and none of us could move even after Medjay Ka-en-Jhutyms pulled the boat single-handedly onto land and dragged each of us all to safety. It was still raining very hard, and I just closed my eyes and passed out.

The next morning, I opened my eyes slowly.

Yes, I thought, *we are still alive on earth.* I touched my face, making sure it was all still there. With amazement, my clothes were dry and hot food lay at my feet with a blazing fire at my back. Medjay Bennu Henenu and Medjay Ni-Sobek were repairing our royal Heru boat, and they had carved two new paddles for our continued journey. Medjay Ka-en-Jhutyms sat next to me, totally relaxed in deep meditation.

"Where is Medjay Sia-en-hotep?" I asked.

Medjay Ni-Sobek replied, "He is looking for the best route around the cataract so we may continue our journey up the Hapy Eteru. We must travel by foot for several more miles." He continued, "It seems that the floodwaters and heavy rains have washed away all the existing trade routes. Please eat, you must regain your strength." Medjay Bennu Henenu gave me a special herb from his pouch.

"This will help," he said softly. I smiled to myself because it seems like all the Medjay were great herbalists.

When Medjay Sia-en-hotep returned, we cleaned up our campsite and gathered together for a prayer before departing.

"May I speak, Medjay Sia-en-hotep?"

"Yes, young Prince Mentchu-hotep," replied Medjay Sia-en-hotep. "I want to thank all of you for saving my life yesterday. It is a miracle

we are all still alive and well. Surely, Amen-Ra and Hapy are watching over us." I fell to my knees in front of Medjay Ka-en-Jhutyms, and I touched and kissed his feet.

"You are a messenger from Amen-Ra himself, and you are surely your father's child. I owe both of you my life ten times over." Uncontrollable tears flooded my eyes. It took several minutes to get control of myself. None of the other Medjay moved.

"Where did you get the strength to do the impossible? What you did was a miracle, great Medjay Ka-en-Jhutyms." At this point, all three of the other Medjay warriors knelt down on one knee and placed one hand on my shoulder. For the first time, I saw tears also in Medjay Bennu Henenu and Medjay Ni-Sobek eyes. It was comforting, knowing that they were still human.

Medjay Ka-en-Jhutyms spoke, "I will tell you what my father told me when I asked him the same question after he saved my life for the third time. There is no order of difficulty in miracles.

One is not harder or bigger than another." He looked into my eyes as he spoke, "You never know how strong you are or can be until being strong is the only choice you have." He paused for a minute, then said, "Amen-Ra has no limits and no boundaries. Once we recognized that Amen-Ra exists in us, then we have no boundary or limits. We are infinite divine spiritual beings having a temporary divine human experience." He took me by my hand and said, "Stand in your own power. Stand with the awareness that you are more than capable of any task. With the conviction that forces are guiding you that you cannot see: ancestors, Ntchru, your own Divine Spirit. Allow yourself to be who you truly are, and walk the path you are destined to walk. Be focused on the vision before you.

"I will share my father's teachings with you and the way of the Medjay. Things that would scare most people to death meant nothing to the chief Medjay Jhutyms Ka-en-Heru because they were nothing to him, and now they are nothing to me. Fear was not a part of the Medjay world. He understood that what we think we see and experience is really a dream, and because you know you are dreaming, you also know that absolutely nothing in the dream could possibly hurt you because none of it was true. You realize you were merely observing symbolic images including people and events that weren't really there. Only the Divine Spirit can guide you, my fellow Medjay spiritual warriors."

He opened his eyes, and I could see that same twinkle I saw in his father's eyes and that I saw in the priest Kha-f-Ptah's eyes.

"I will repeat it again," he said. "You will come to know and experience that the Ntchr is not outside of you. When that happens, you will no longer identify yourself with a vulnerable body or anything else that can be limited. You will learn instead of your true reality as pure spirit that is invulnerable forever."

"Dwa Ntchr." We all spoke as one voice repeating, "Dwa Ntchr!" We all spent a minute or two just hugging each other, and I was so thankful because I knew they were doing this for me.

As we began our journey, I insisted that I help carry the boat. And finally, Medjay Ka-en-Jhutyms nodded his head, and my wish was granted. We walked silently for about twenty minutes as Medjay Sia-en- hotep led the way, and then above my head, I saw two men tied, gagged, and strapped to a very large tree. I know the other Medjay saw it also, but they did not say a word or even acknowledged their presence, so I just kept moving. Finally, after about two hours, we reconnected with Hapy Eteru, the mighty river. My arms and shoulders were even happier than I was to see Hapy.

We met an elder along the shore. Medjay Sia-en-hotep said something to him in a language I did not understand, then he gave him a bag.

After his conversation with the elder, he said to us that we would rest there for a minute and for Medjay Bennu to relieve me. I wanted to say no, but my arms and shoulders took control, and I just nodded my head with approval.

"We must still walk another hour up south because the current is still too strong for our vessel," Medjay Sia-en-hotep said. After a very short rest, we continued on our journey. We walked without seeing another living soul for about an hour before the royal Heru boat regained harmony with the great Hapy Eteru. We reached the trade city of Khartoum just before nightfall, looking into a beautiful Ra Set. On the third day, this was where the two great rivers met to become one. This in itself was a wonder to behold, but I didn't have the energy or strength to enjoy it for the second time. As we approached the city, another royal Ankh Medjay boat met us and escorted us to a Medjay training camp nearby.

Great! Food, water, and some real rest, I thought.

That evening, I asked Medjay Ni-Sobek about the two men tied to the tree I saw when we were walking around the cataract earlier that day.

Medjay Ni-Sobek smiled and said, "They were two thieves who tried to rob Medjay Sia-en-hotep, so he taught them a little lesson. He paid the elderly man we saw at the river to cut them loose with the weapons he took from them." We both laughed.

"You have to be crazy, trying to rob a Medjay," I said. We laughed again for a long time as we sat around the campfire with several other Medjay.

We stayed at this Medjay camp for two weeks, and my major lesson here was keeping my balance on the papyrus boats while navigating Hapy. By the fifth day, I had gotten pretty good, I thought, until I saw Medjay Ka-en-Jhutyms do a complete spear and long pole form on the papyrus boat in perfect balance with Hapy while three other Medjay warriors were trying to strike him with their poles. This by itself was pure magic. On the tenth day, one week later, they added the throwing sticks into the program. On land, I was pretty good with the throwing sticks, but standing on the papyrus boats bobbing up and down in the waters of Hapy, that was a different scenario altogether. I couldn't hit an elephant while throwing these sticks standing in the boat as long as Hapy was in control.

Medjay warriors practicing pole fighting

Medjay Ka-en-Jhutyms saw my dilemma. He pulled me to the side and said, "Watch," as he stood on one leg inside a bobbing papyrus boat. "You must forget about the boat, forget about Hapy, and imagine they don't exist, which they don't. Remember, you are the captain of your own ship, and your existence shares the same harmonious reality of Ma'at. You are urged to develop a relationship with the Divine Spirit. It will inspire the mind and expand the consciousness, thereby, bringing to you more and more the awareness of yourself as a spiritual being. And as a conscious spiritual being, there is nothing you can't do. Now throw the sticks like you were on land and as though the sticks and the target occupy the same space at the same time, and you can't miss."

He hit the target five times in a row, the last two with his eyes closed. "Do you understand?" he said to me.

"How do you see in the dark or blindfolded, Master?"

"The physical world is an aggregate of frequencies. Each chemical element is uniquely identifiable in the electromagnetic spectrum by its own unique set of separately unique frequencies like fingerprints.

"We have all some electrical and magnetic forces within us, and we put forth, like a magnet itself, an attractive or repulsive power as we come in contact with something similar or dissimilar. The truth is, everything is alive, and everything is receiving and giving off energy. Life is not just a material substance. Life is a force, and it is electrical and magnetic—a quality, not a quantity. We must learn to feel this electromagnetic force with our heart and our consciousness. The intellect is powerless to express thought without the help of the heart. It is only with the heart that one can see rightly, what is essential is invisible to the eye. A warrior unable to see light as anything other than a purely physical phenomenon will be blind to light and to a Medjay's attack." "I will work on it, Neb." I thought, *Tiw, through several lifetimes I' ll still be working on this one.*

"I heard that Medjay Mentchu-hotep and you will accomplish this task in this lifetime. What really counts are the upward and forward progress and commitment to improve," he said as he walked away without looking back.

I said to myself, *even my own thoughts are not mine alone but part of the collective. I have to watch even what I think. He is surely his father's child.* On the last day, we were packed and ready to go but not before visiting the great market in the city of Khartoum. It was one of the largest trading centers I had ever seen before, larger than anything in Kemet. Excitement was everywhere with all the different traders from all over, some traveling for hundreds of miles with their goods. I saw men seven feet tall and men three feet short. There were many different nations of people here. Every shade of black and brown on the color spectrum was represented in their different complexions. I even saw several rare albino men. I felt myself staring at one market woman. She was reddish brown in skin color from the land of Punt, and she had black henna writing all over her face, arms, hands, legs, and feet. She looked like a painting. In addition, any kind of animal that existed in our lands near or far could also be bought and sold here. I was impressed for the second time because I had been here with the chief of the Medjay warriors, Medjay Jhutyms Ka-en-Heru, three years earlier.

Before our two-day travel to the capital of Meroe, Barwat, also the home of the Medjay, we were honored with the presence of the great chief of the Medjay warriors, Medjay Jhutyms Ka-en-Heru. He was not only the father to Medjay Ka-en-Jhutyms and Medjay Akhtoy Ba-Heru, but he was honored as all our spiritual fathers. We looked up to him with great adoration for he was the greatest of all living Medjay and the greatest living warrior on earth and heaven. Some 250 or more Medjay gathered around Medjay Jhutyms Ka-en-Heru as he spoke.

"Before I talk about this common illusion that we share as a nation, I want you, mighty Medjay warriors, to know you are mighty spirits connected to the one Divine Spirit. You are far greater than you think. What you see me do, you are capable of doing and even far greater things. People are spirits. They just don't know it. And how can you really be a person if you're not a body? And you are not your body. In Barwat, I will explain the mind and the ego, but now it is nation time." "Come closer, mighty Medjay, we are in the land of Meroe. Some of you, my courageous brothers, come from Napata and Kerma. We welcome you. And a few of you come from as far north as Kemet, our beloved land, we welcome you all. Kemet, Kerma, and Napata are all located in the dry desert where the narrow Hapy Valley has limited cultivation. Meroe, like Punt and Ta Ntchr, on the other hand, lay in the well-watered triangle of land between the Hapy Eteru and the Atbara Eteru. Because of its location, outsiders called it the Island of Meroe."

Laughter came from the Medjay. "In the northern part of Kash, it scarcely rains, but Meroe lay within a southern region of tropical seasonal rainfall. We have taken advantage of the climate and have built large rain collection pools and a complex system of irrigation canals. Fields could be cultivated some distance away from Hapy, not depending on the Hapy floods. We could grow in abundance sorghum and mille, grains, beans, and a large variety of fruits and, in some cases, have two crops a year. Cattle and other livestock could graze on the grasslands. There is also good hunting because game is plentiful here.

So you can see, my Medjay brothers, why we are a powerful nation and the homeland and parents to our northern brothers and sisters.

"But the real reasons, my family, that we are great are three things. Our iron ore—yes, the ability to craft the art of smelting iron for superior tools and weapons. Our central government, with the Shemsu Heru as an absolute monarch just as in Kemet. But we Meroites enjoy greater political freedom than our brothers and sisters in Kemet. The selection of our Shemsu Heru requires the consent of nobles and priests, and an unpopular ruler could be removed. Ma'at was developed here, and no one is exempted from Ma'at—not even the Shemsu Heru or his royal family. We are the founders of Shemsu Heru. Our royal mother or Nswt Mwt Wrt, great royal Mwt, is held in high esteem and controls greater power than in Kemet. The third reason we have become a great nation is trade and the control of trade." He took a long drink of water. "Meroe is ideally located for the development of international trade.

Just north of the second cataract, traders could cut across the desert to rejoin the Hapy Eteru above the fifth cataract, thus, avoiding treacherous stretches of the Hapy Eteru in between. It can be treacherous. I'm sure my son, Medjay Ka-en-Jhutyms, and his small group with Prince Mentchu-hotep have witnessed this. In fact, I'm willing to believe we all have encountered its ruggedness at some point in our lives." The whole group nodded in agreement.

"From the fifth cataract, you could travel downstream into Kemet, one of our biggest customers and trade partners.

"Hapy Eteru also takes us south to Ta Ntchr, the foothills to the mountains of the moon. There lay the great savannas and the tropical rain forest. Several routes extended east to the Ymnsqt, the Red Sea, where we could trade with the people of the Wedjy Wr [Mediterranean], southern Arabia, India, Punt, Chaldea, Sumer, Persia, the whole eastern coast of Asia, and the far east. Finally, my Medjay warriors, the great west across the western desert and mountains to Lake Chad and regions of the great western rain forest. Our iron weapons and tools for mining, hunting, and farming helped Meroites to provide trade goods such as ivory, leopard skins, ostrich feathers and eggs, gold, and ebony wood. We also supplied iron implements for sale in distant markets. And I save the best for last, my great Medjay warriors. None of this would be possible if it were not for the great Medjay warriors who act as the guardians of Ma'at."

All the Medjay stood up and cheered long and hard. "This is why we must train harder than anyone else." The Medjay yelled, "Dwa Ntchr!"

"This is why we Medjay must prevail."

All the Medjay together yelled, "Dwa Ntchr!"

After we all calmed down, chief of the Medjay warriors, Medjay Jhutyms Ka-en-Heru, spoke again, "Tonight we are going to initiate our newest group of courageous warriors into the Medjay brothership."

The Medjay cheered like thunder.

"Come forward, Napatian warrior Kames. Come forward, Kerma warrior Meket-Ra. Come forward, Ta Ntchr warrior Simba. And come forward, my Kemet warrior crown prince Mentchu-hotep."

The Medjay crowd cheered and yelled again even louder. I was shocked. I thought it would take me another two years just to start initiation. We danced around the campfire for hours as the drums roared like thunder in the hands of Medjay master musicians. Medjay Ka-en-Jhutyms and Medjay Akhtoy Ba-Heru danced with their father as they did some kind of form to the element of fire together in perfect harmony. Ka-en-Jhutyms and Medjay Akhtoy Ba-Heru twirled and leaped into the air, defying the laws of gravity and heat. The whole camp was in a frenzy. Medjay Jhutyms Ka-en-Heru picked up several pieces of hot coals with his bare hands without being burned. In fact, fire was blazing from his hands as he rolled the flames up into a fireball. The whole crowds of Medjay were mesmerized as he leaped into the air, twisting and twirling the fireball around his body, then with a great force, he threw the fireball into the campfire. And the flames swelled to ten feet high, and everyone near the fire jumped back from the intensity of the heat. And then like a mighty lion, Medjay Jhutyms Ka-en-Heru spun around and thrust his open empty hands toward the flames, and instantaneously, the fire was out.

I couldn't sleep at all that night, and I revisited my journey with the chief of the Medjay warriors, Medjay Jhutyms

Ka-en-Heru, and all his lessons in our two-and-half-year journey. Only now was I beginning to understand what he was trying to convey to me: that even in the eye of a mighty storm, there is peace, and you must find that peace under or in any condition. This is how Medjay Ka-en-Jhutyms was able to save us. We got caught up in the illusion of the confusion of the flooding turbulent waters that did not exist, but Medjay Ka-en-Jhutyms found his inner peace and the source of his power, the Divine Spirit, and used it to save our lives.

I could even hear the chief Medjay's voice saying to me, "Start at the very core of who *you* are, your mind. Learn to love yourself and to forgive yourself. Be at peace with it. Honor it. Defend it. Express it. Share it. This is where you'll discover the source of your power. This is the home of the Divine Spirit. This is where the ancestors and your great-grandfather Shemsu Heru Mentchu-hotep will speak to you. And this is where you'll find the answers that you've been looking for. Always have faith in the Divine Spirit in *you*, Crown Prince Mentchu-hotep." My mission was much clearer now with my expanded consciousness.

My relationship with myself helped me also understand the great Hapy Eteru. I had to be deliberate and focused like the Hapy Eteru. It has purpose as it flows from its source, but it has adaptability and is always in motion. It may take ten thousand to one million years, but it carves its way through whatever gets in its path—whatever or whoever. Hapy Eteru is methodical, driven, forceful, unified, and often even overflowing their banks with raging waters, then subsiding but never stopping until the source one day runs dry. The chief Medjay said we could learn a lot from studying the Hapy Eteru. I can see what my father, Intef Sa Ra, Shemsu Heru Nakht-neb-tep-nefer, wanted for me and for Kemet. His father and he and his brothers could not unite Kemet, and he knew that our northern foes were growing very powerful from joining with Asian allies. He knew the type of strength, power, and leadership that was necessary to unite all of Kemet and to maintain our sovereignty like the first Shemsu Heru warriors who came from the south, and that is why I am here.

CHAPTER 5

THE INITIATION

When we arrived at the main Medjay village and training camp in Medja, a village on the southeast corner of Barwat, I was pleasantly surprised again. There was new construction with several new temples since my last visit, especially the temple of Amen-Ra. The Meroites and Kashites worshipped and gave homage to many of the same Ntchru as we did in Kemet, and they had a profound understanding of the principles and laws of nature and the solar system, as well as the cosmos. Astronomy and astrology, the study of Heru's vision was born here. I could clearly see that we influenced each other as many of our traditions came from here, some were refined and improved and yet other cultural traditions Kemet created and influenced Kash. The Hem Ntchr Tepy Dagi of the Amen Temple knew this, and so did my father, the lifeline of Kemet. Ta Mry (the beloved land) came from the south.

My Medjay initiation was completed at the sacred temple of Amen-Ra in Barwat. The Hem Ntchr Tepy here was a Medjay, and I recognized him at first glance. He was the third Medjay fighter at the homecoming ceremony of the return of Chief Medjay Jhutyms Ka-en- Heru and myself to Kemet almost three and a half years ago. He was the one who defeated the Asiatic giant in two moves. How impressive. I could still see the reruns of that battle in my head as I glanced into his eyes. He moved like Medjay Ka-en-Jhutyms and Chief Medjay Jhutyms Ka-en-Heru. I was beginning to recognize a subtle twinkle in their eyes that is not found even in the most powerful of warriors. This is the twinkle that scared my little sister, Princess Neferu. I will train extra hard. I must find the source of that twinkle.

At the conclusion of our initiate entrance ceremony after we had demonstrated our Mentchu and Medjay combat skills—boxing, grappling, animal dance and forms, weaponry, and all the Ma'at Akhu

Ba Ankh (Kemet-Kash breathing and meditative postures). Next were the cultural and healing components—music, drumming and dance, food, herbs, healing touch, and acupressure. Next were the spiritual and ourstorical components. We had to know the way of spiritual consciousness, the way of spiritual works, the way of spiritual knowledge, the way of spiritual devotion, and the way of spiritual Mrr (love). Finally, toward the end of initiation, we had to demonstrate the way of spiritual and earthly forgiveness. We then had to explain the way of the warrior and the meaning behind our pledge.

After we talked about the power behind positive affirmations, we recited the ten virtues of an initiate:

1. *Control of thoughts.* Learn to mediate so that you can control the way you think, as well as what you think. Analyze every situation before you react. You must be a warrior for Ma'at, which is to bring about order if there is none.

2. *Control of actions.* Each spiritual warrior is in the process of mastering their thoughts so they can create the right

thinking. In order for the spiritual warrior to influence others, they must consistently produce the right action.

3. *Steadfastness of purpose.* Staying power. If you believe with all your heart in the mission, then you must have fortitude. Being steadfast is holding to your Medjay and Kemetic principles.

4. *Identify with spiritual life or higher ideas based on Ma'at.* We are Divine Spirit in a divine human form. This is our first and foremost identity. Our identity must be with our ancestors, the Medjay, and the spirit of Kemet and Kash for eternity.

5. *Evidence of having a mission in life.* The Maangamizi speaks of a need to liberate ourselves. Ma'at is our mission in life. The development of our gifts is the vehicle, which will help us accomplish our mission.

6. *Evidence of wanting to be a Medjay.* Once you have seen the mission and understand its importance, then you must move in that direction. And the only direction that can liberate us is toward becoming a spiritual Medjay warrior.

7. *Freedom from resentment when under the experience of persecution.* With Heru consciousness comes enlightenment. One who is enlightened sees change as a must because the alternative is death for our people and the way of our ancestors—mentally, physically, and spiritually. Now comes the conflict as your parents, family, and friends don't see and can't see what you see. You can't follow their path, and they don't see yours. They will act negatively toward you as you follow your mission as a spiritual Medjay warrior. Only courage

will help you stay on the path of Ma'at, and this great courage comes from within. This courage will keep you from being resentful against those who don't see, and that same courage will stop their resentment from getting in you and slowing you down.

8. *Confidence in the power of Medjay warrior masters and Kemet and Kash priest scientist.* If you have come to the level where you want to develop or change, then the best thing to do is to become the student of someone more advance in the path of mastery in your field. Do your research and make sure you are following a master teacher who is someone who has demonstrated their attachment to Ma'at through their actions, not just words and that they are a spiritual Medjay warrior for our people of Kemet, Kash, Napata, and Meroe.

9. *Confidence in one's own ability to learn.* The greatest teacher cannot teach unless the student is willing to change. The only thing that prevents change is the unwillingness to change. Change is the only consistent quality in the cosmos.

10. *Readiness or preparedness for initiation.* When the student is ready, the master will appear. The receipt of knowledge is worthless unless change follows. We must be prepared to change and grow into spiritual Medjay warriors.

For the next year, I would remain at the Medjay headquarters in Barwat, training in the ways of the Medjay as a spiritual warrior. Our schedule was eight days of training and two days off for rest and reflection. This was a week in the Kemet and Kash calendar system—ten days in a week, three weeks in a month, thirty days in each month with twelve months, equaling 360 days. The twelve months had three seasons with four months in each season. Inundation was the first season, called Shemu. The second season was called Peret, the growing season. And the third season was called Akhet, the harvest season. Kemet and Kash also had a thirteenth month, which only had five days called five days above the year. These five days were a time of celebration, giving thanks for what we have and the Ntchru, sharing our harvest but preparing for the New Year. The five Ntchru were Asr, Ast, Heru Ur, Setsh, and Nebet-Het. About six months after my initiation, my mother's brother had passed. He was Intef Aa Sa Ra, Heru Wah-ankh, and he was the royal treasurer for twenty years. He was very close to my parents, and he was from the sacred city of Abu, southern Kemet. During his post, he managed to expand trade with Kash, bringing new ideas and commerce to Kemet, and expanded trade northward to the city of Iwenet. I knew my family needed me more than ever to be strong. I did not return home for his Asarian ceremony, returning him home in the west. Instead I intensified my training and dedicated that extra day in prayer to my family. My family was not happy about this, especially my little sister, Neferu. But I was focused, and I did not want any distractions especially since I knew it was an illusion anyway. The resurrection is something that happens in your mind and has nothing to do with your body. He was not his body. He was spirit, and we were one. One evening while I was sitting in meditation, he, Heru Wah-ankh, came to me and told me how proud he was of me and that he understood my mission. I was clear about the power of the soul, which was an aspect of the one Divine Spirit, and my training grew by leaps and bounds. And then I only took one day off each week from that point on.

On one of my reflection days, I was reviewing my notes on the ego, and I wanted to make sure I understood these profound teachings. Chief Medjay Jhutyms Ka-en-Heru said that the ego is nothing more than a part of your belief about yourself that exists in your mind. And this ego is a master illusionist. You are not your body. Your body is an illusion created by the ego. You are spirit, and you are not disconnected from the Creator. There is only oneness, and duality is an illusion created by the ego. The Ntchr is. And nothing exists outside of the Ntchr. The chief Medjay said you must learn how to choose between the Divine Spirit who represents the real you and the part of your mind that represents the false you created by the ego. By studying with the Medjay, you will learn how to do it in such a way that your long-imprisoned unconscious mind can finally be freed. It is almost impossible to do this on your own. As my light grew, I could see the light in others. All relationships provide an opportunity for the Divine Spirit to flow to and through us. When the creative divine flows from us, it connects with its kind in others, and the resulting contact produces greater light. When the heart beats with a rhythm of cosmic love and the head vibrates with cosmic wisdom, a connection is made with Ntchr and the Divine Spirit.

I began to see myself and imagine myself and visualize myself each day as a lighted being of cosmic light and love. I could see cosmic light and love descending to and through myself as I held still within this light, absorbing, reflecting, and transmitting its energies.

The chief Medjay Jhutyms Ka-en-Heru also said that the state of being more seemingly awake in the dream is what passes for enlightenment among the masses who are asleep and unaware of the dream. These enlightened beings have always been here because the ego cannot fool all the so-called people all the time. The so-called history or even ourstory of the universe and specifically the world—past, present, and future—is simply a script that was written by the ego. The so-called past, present, and future are all occurring simultaneously, but in reality, they do not exist. Only Ntchr exists. Since there is really no separation from the one, the Creator or the Ntchr, there is no guilt or original sin. This is why completely guiltless minds like a Medjay spiritual priest or spiritual grand master would never suffer pain. Because there is no pain, there is no body and there is no world. It's possible for regular Medjay who are not masters to alleviate their pain also and do countless remarkable things with their minds on the road to becoming masters. I must make a footnote that this is where I need more clarification. I can see even in my group, we have Medjay who are not masters, yet they can perform what we call as miracles.

Each journey that I went on now always consisted of a unit of *medju* (ten) Medjay warriors. The Hem Ntchr Tepy in Kemet as well as in Meroe said that ten Medjay warriors were equal to one hundred or more regular well-trained solders. Medjay Ka-en-Jhutyms added five more Medjay warriors to our team after my initiation, giving us the unit of Medjay Medju. One of the magnificent young warriors was from Punt, and he was the younger brother of Medjay Ka-en-Jhutyms, and two of these new Medjay were born and raised in the village of Medja in Barwat. Even though they were young—around the age of Medjay Ka- en-Jhutyms, maybe early twenties—each one's skills matched Medjay Sia-en-hotep. One evening after training, I asked Medjay Hu-Sia, the Hem Ntchr Tepy of the Barwat temple of Amen-Ra, about the level of skills among the new Medjay warriors on my new Medjay *medju* team under the direction of Medjay Ka-en-Jhutyms.

My question was, "Hem Sem Tepy Medjay Hu-Sia, these five new Medjay are just a little older than myself, but yet their skills are equal to our senior Medjay who belongs to Chief Medjay Jhutyms Ka-en-Heru's elite team of Medjay. How can this be?" I asked. "Three of them have mastered skills that take at least fifteen to twenty years to master, but they are in their early twenties."

He thought for a moment, then he spoke, "It has to do with bloodline. These Medjay all are descendants of the original Medjay family who came here three great floods ago."

"How long ago was that?" I asked. "Maybe 250,000 years ago." "Came here from where?" I asked.

"I can answer that only because you are also part of our bloodline. Your great-great-grandmother was one of us, Ikui. She was a legendary Medjay warrior, and your great-grandfather, Mentchu-hotep, was her son, who was a full Medjay. And you are named after him. It was he, your great-grandfather, who founded and reestablished the royal family at Waset during the time of confusion. Why do you think you were chosen by Medjay Jhutyms Ka-en-Heru to come here?"

"I thought it was my father's request," I said.

"No, even the Shemsu Heru from Kemet, now the most powerful nation on your planet, has no power over the Medjay."

"What do you mean my planet? Don't you mean our planet?" "You better sit down," Medjay Hu-Sia said.

"We, each of us, are intricately connected to the larger universe. It is our true home, and thinking that this physical world we call Geb [earth] is all that matters is like shutting oneself up in a small room and imagining that there is nothing else out beyond it. This other vastly grander universe isn't far away at all. It is right here where I am. It is right there where you are but simply exists on a different frequency."

The crown prince had a puzzled look on his face as he spoke. "You kind of lost me at the end there. I thought the universe was an illusion. So what are you talking about?"

"You will learn or have learned that the universe, which you called an illusion is held together by consciousness, and this consciousness gave birth to the cosmos that is the billions of galaxies. And all of these galaxies have consciousness." He paused for a moment and then continued, "The mind has many dimensions to it. We are operating on the third dimension right now as we talk. Some of the miracles that you have seen have occurred on the fourth dimension. I am connected to beings that come from the fifth dimension. All these dimensions appear to be happening at the same time. One thought made all images appear because they all represent the same thing in seemingly different forms and different dimensions."

This is getting deep, I thought to myself.

"On the fifth dimension, the planet that our common ancestors came from was destroyed. We were light energy beings, and the sun that controlled our planet turned into a supernova. One of the most energetic explosive events known is a supernova. This occurs at the end of a star's lifetime when its nuclear fuel is exhausted and it is no longer supported by the release of nuclear energy. If the star is particularly massive, then its core will collapse and, in so doing, will release a huge amount of energy. This will cause a blast wave that ejects the star's envelope into interstellar space. The result of the collapse may be, in some cases, a rapidly rotating neutron star that can be observed many years later as a radio pulsar. In Kemet, you called one of those stars Spdt snu or Sirius B, and it lays behind the star Spdt, the Dog Star or Sirius A, the brightest star in your visible night sky."

"I have read about this star in my studies, and I have seen the illusion of it in the night sky. And I know that it brings forth our New Year, but no one mentioned life coming from there," I said.

Medjay Hu-Sia continued, "Groups of us escaped and flew with our advanced technology to other parts of the cosmos in search of a new home. Our ancestors were part of the free moving, free acting, and free choosing intelligent souls in the universe created by the One Big Mind. The semiphysical and the nonphysical beings from our planet merged together into one being and asked permission from your galaxy we call the Milky Way and then from your solar system, headed by Ra, which also has a consciouness. We asked permission from your solar system, Ra, to come here, the third planet from Ra. This disruption in the universe even caused most of the so-called life in your solar system, like from Mars and the moon and on this planet's surface, to become extinct. In many of the planets in this solar system, life never returned."

"You mean other live beings on other planets?" I asked.

"*Tiw,* hundreds of thousands of other life forms even in the Milky way even as we speak."

A supernova explosion in action

"When we came here, there were six humanoid life forms and three reptilian life forms of free-moving, free-acting, free-choosing intelligent souls of high intelligence that the mind could comprehend. The reptilian life forms lived underground and in deep caves because they could not handle the ultraviolet rays from Ra or the direct light energy also coming from Ra. Other alien beings from the dark side of a few nearby planets also came to Earth not long after us. They crossed their own DNA with that of certain reptiles and reptilians, and many of those creatures are still here also. A few of them can shape-shift, appearing to look humanlike. It was also from these creatures that the reptilian [dragon] beings of the Asiatic stories were born."

"Wait, are you trying to tell me that dragons are real?"

"*Tiw*, but because they, the dragons, were a threat to the original human life and our own existence on the planet, we, the Medjay warriors, hunted them down and destroyed them all. We allowed the other reptilians to live, but they were no longer allowed to enter this continent in search of gold, food, or slaves or interfere with life on the surface here."

"You mean they were here in our homeland?"

"*Tiw*, they came for gold and other natural resources that are abundant here. If you go farther south, you will see traces of their gold mines and corrals and export stations, and some still exist underground. Most of the gold-exploring alien beings left. The reptilians stayed in Asia along with their crossbreeds. They drink blood, and some ate animal and human flesh to live. These reptilians and crossbreeds drink and eat the person's life force because they need this to exist in this dimension on this planet and to maintain their human form. These reptilians and their crossbreeds lack the fully formed emotional and spiritual level of the original human beings, which are activated by Ra through your pineal gland and dark skin color called melanin. Didn't you notice that most Asians and northerners are extremely aggressive?"

Medjay Mentchu-hotep spoke, "I read that they have been fighting since the time of Heru and have never known peace."

"The saying goes, lo! The vile Aamu, wretched is the place, which he is from. Suffering from hidden waters with barren trees and many dangerous paths because of the mountains. He is not from one place only. His legs walk about, circling. He has been fighting since the time of Heru, yet he does not conquer, nor is he conquered. He does not announce the day of fighting like a robber who returns to the pack."

He looked into my eyes and said, "Are things getting cleared now?" He continued, "Their works and their values reflect aggression. Their primitive technology is aggression directed against the natural world. Their military technology is aggression directed against their fellow human beings. And much of their art and culture reflects sexual aggression. They have war among their own sexes. These Asiatic northerners, because of their hairy nature, their sexes have never really gotten used to each other and never trusted each other. And so they, these reptilians, and another group of visiting beings called Oannes and the Annunaki by the Sumerians and their crossbreeds use mind control and programmed humans of particular bloodlines, like recessive aggressive Asiatic humans who have a calcified pineal gland and who lack melanin, to perform the rituals and draw in the energies for them that they need to survive here on earth. These Asiatic humans were more beastlike and were driven into the cold climates of the north by our Medjay warrior ancestors where they still exist as we talk. They have migrated out of the mountains and caves slowly since the end of the last ice age and are the source of much of your planets confusion and problems today."

"So if we are the people of Ra, the sun, they are people of the ice and caves," said Medjay Mentchu-hotep.

"*Tiw,* our ancestors, the spiritual beings from Spdt snu, mixed our DNA with these original melaninated humans who were already millions of years old and who had mastered nature and had a very peaceful nature, not like their Asiatic cousins, the northern and western Asiatics. We needed this Twa, San, Khui, and Anu knowledge to survive here on this planet. Today we are the off shoots of the Twa, San, Khui, and Anu Bush indigenous black and brown people of this continent, Ta Khenset. For millenniums of equatorial existence, we fused not only our DNA, but also our souls together with these original Ra people of the tropical belt of this planet. Our advanced wisdom and technology taught us to learn to become one with your environment. Do not try to change the wind or the sea, change the sails."

"These new beings became the Annu during their golden age of development. Our first ancestors here gave the scribes of the Annu the Emerald Tablets and the forty-two books of Jhuty on this planet."

"I have had the honor of studying some of these great works," said Medjay Mentchu-hotep.

"All of the Shemsu Heru must in order to lead and know the way," said the Hem Sem Tepy Hu-Sia. "But later you also must study the cuneiform tablets of Inky and the Annunaki." He continued, "With this advance spiritual information and technology, we developed several great golden ages on this planet. There is evidence of these civilizations in southern

Asia, the South Pacific islands, Turtle Island, and in the tropical belt to the far west called Atlantis and Lamuria and here in southern Afraka.

"But also during this time, great changes were taking place on the earth's surface, causing the physical destruction of many of these great golden ages and our advanced way of life. Once again we survived and came back to the Hapy Valley. Heru em Akhety and several ancient temples in Kemet are more than thirty thousand years old from a previous golden age and have survived the last great flood.

"This whole continent is a plateau, high above sea level and is one of the most stable places on earth. The ruins of these great golden ages can still be found underwater or buried under the tropical rain forest on several continents today. There still exist great underground tunnels and cities and sacred landing ports above ground for other intelligent life forces. All of these places are sacred spaces that connect many of these great power points on your planet's energy grid. Even the great pyramids of Snefru and Khufu were built on top of sacred structures from other golden ages before the last Great Flood."

"How long ago was this last great flood?" I asked.

"Remember, time is an illusion, but according to your imaginary records around nine thousand years ago, Ta, the Earth's sea level rose suddenly more than twenty meters [about sixty-six feet] in less than two hundred years. This was the direct result of catastrophic glacial melting that heralded the beginning of an eight-thousand-year period called the end of the last ice age when sea levels rose 120 meters [almost four hundred feet] essentially to the level they are today. And that's why Heru m Akhety has water erosion on it, and the great ruins in Ta Ntchr and southern Afraka were even underwater. This flood destroyed almost 85 percent of the world's population.

"If and when you become a Medjay priest-scientist, you will be able to access the Askashic records, the human mass consciousness, and the karma. Knowledge of the planet and solar system will be revealed to you. When your spiritual and electrical power is much greater, you can enter this morphic field, then you will know that yesterday and tomorrow are all happening now. As this planet changes its consciousness, we have to evolve and change with it in order to survive here.

"I will ask more questions later about these Askashic records," said Medjay Mentchu-hotep.

"Of course, the ability to clearly see the past is one of the best tools the Askashic records have to offer us. If you can view the past without attachment, you can make wiser changes to your script of life. You are the director of your play. Where was I?

"*Tiw*, there was a dispute over how the Emerald Tablets and forty- two books of Jhuty were to be used by the survivors of the last great flood about seven thousand years ago, so we split into two major groups and a few subgroups who left our continent. Since the last great flood, the order of evidence for civilizations is Hapy Eteru Valley, Indus River Valley, Tigris-Euphrates River, and Shang [Yellow] River. What you see in ancient and present day Kemet, Kash, Napata, Meroe, Punt, Kilwa, Zimbabwe, the Niger River, the Kongo River, and in the southern part of this continent were the scientists, astrologists, and engineers who built temples and statues and who mastered the natural crystal energy of this planet. We developed the Mdw Ntchr as an expression of our love and understanding of this environment."

The Hem Sem Tepy Hu-Sia took a long drink of water, then continued, "The second group was the Medjay, who became warriors, traders, explorers, and peace administrators of Ma'at. So the first Shemsu Heru was Heru Bes since the last Great Flood. Chief Medjay Bes traveled and civilized all of the known civilized parts of this continent, Ta Ntchr, with his advance knowledge and use of iron."

"Wait, I was told the first king was Asr."

"And you are right, Asr was a ruler and high priest, but not a warrior under the chief Medjay Bes. Just like Narmer was a ruler under Chief Medjay Annu Aa, and your father is the fourth ruler of Kemet, but the chief Medjay is Jhutyms Ka-en-Heru."

"*Tiw*, I understand now."

"The second chief Medjay was Memnon, ruler of all Kash. There are many of our people here in Meroe who are called Memnones after our great chief Medjay Memnon. I believe you met one of their priests in Napata, Priest Kha-f-Ptah, the head architect of the city of Napata, a deep soul. During the rule of Memnon, this is where the split came about. It was Memnon that left Kash and seized the whole coast of Arabia and Libya, southern India and then went on and founded Susa, the chief city of the Elamites. He was also the leader of the Black Heads or the black-faced people who founded Sumeria. These Kashite Sumerians were the inventors of the cuneiform system of writing, which was later adopted by their Semitic conquers. The major difference between these two writing systems was cuneiform was totally abstract and was used only by the ruling priest, the royal families, and the common people never learned it. Other space travelers like the Annunaki who came here for the gold communicated their story in cuneiform to our ancestors. So the Chaldeans, Acadians, southern Indians called Dravidians, the southern Sumerians were all colonies of the vast Kashite empire. Memnon is sometimes called the great falcon. That is why all the Sumeria, Chaldean, and Persian leaders, all their kings were depicted as falcon-headed men. And Memnon, he ruled for almost three hundred years before his great son took the throne."

The founders of the first Mesopotamian civilization were black Sumerians, sun folks. Mesopotamia was the biblical land of Shinar (Sumer), which sprung up around three thousand BCE. The founders of the civilization were of Kashite (Cushite) origin. It's clear by many anthropologists that the Semitic speakers of Akkad and the non-Semitic speakers of Sumer were both black people who called themselves sag-gig-ga or Black Heads, and like Kemet, their rulers were great falcons.

"Memnon's legendary son was Nimrod, who was later called the son of Kash. It was Nimrod who built the great temple of Asut and which is the great tower of Babylon. Nimrod and Hercules are one and the same. *The Epic of the Adventures of Nimrod* was preserved in the library at Erich and is identical with the twelve labors of Hercules. The passage of Hercules represents the early colonization of western Asia by Kash. It becomes confusing sometimes to foreigners because just like you have the name of your grandfather, so did Memnon and Nimrod.

"Also the name Belus or Bolus is also a son of Nimrod, the king of Chaldea who built the famous Temple of Anu and connected Susiana, Persia, Media, and southern India to the original Kashite family. Nimrod was also called the legendary black panther or the black bird, and his children founded the first Shang dynasty, civilizing China, the Mongols, and the Far East."

Chief Annu Aa, the fourth chief Medjay and father of Medjay Jhutyms Ka-en- Heru. Iwnyt-Hwt-miew-Hmn-tr-nTr / hall of pillars. Temple of the Cat. City of Hemen. Worshipper of the Ntchr. (Early dynastic period before the reign of Narmer.)

Ȧn Rā , the Ȧnu of Rā.

"Medjay Narmer was the eleventh warrior priest of the fourth Shemsu Heru of the reunification of our people after the last Great Flood. He had belonged to a group of Kashite priest rulers who were followers of one of our chief Medjay called Annu Aa, our fourth chief Medjay. Chief Medjay Jhutyms Ka-en-Heru is our fifth chief Medjay since Heru Bes, and he has been chief for more than 175 years."

"What?" I said in disbelief. "People ruling for 250 and 300 years, this is stretching it of course, right?"

"Nn, I would not do that. I can only share Ma'at with you. I am the Hem Sem Tepy of Amen-Ra."

"Are you trying to tell me that the chief Medjay Jhutyms Ka-en- Heru is 175 years old when he looks maybe 45 at most?" I said.

"He's older than that. I said he has been ruling for 175 years. Before the last Great Flood, we lived for thousands of years. But your world is getting smaller, and we have to share energies. So we agreed, with the new energy consciousness on this planet, on a three-hundred-year rulership as our new limit. Remember, there is no time. Everything, which is nothing, is happening now."

"Now you know you have to explain that. Is time real or not?" "Time is also an illusion. You will learn that the so-called sin or giant explosion equals a separation mentally from the one, creating the illusion of duality, which does not exist. This illusion is equal to the past. The guilt of the separation within the duality, which does not exist, is equal to the present. And fear, which does not exist, equals the future. Remember, everything is happening in the mind, and your mind is ageless because time isn't real."

"One second, wait, I can't even use that word since time does not exist. So just tell me the truth, Ma'at, what is the so-called difference between our two Medjay bloodlines?"

"How we think. We know this is an illusion, so we think symptomatically, not symbolically. Your mind has accepted the illusion as real, and your ego rules your mind with symbols and mythology, which is a fairy tale inside the dream—superstitions, which in many cases are based upon nothing or a lie.

"The Medjay you asked about, also including myself, are all direct descendants from our first ancient ancestor's bloodline who came here 250,000 years ago. They all have two unmixed Medjay parents and only think symptomatically versus one or two Medjay parent mixed in with the blood of the indigenous human like yourself who think symbolically.

"I hope I am clarifying much of the confusion around civilizations. Culture is not necessarily civilization. The first hominids had cultures, so too did *Homo erectus* and *Homo hablis.* Even cavemen and the Aamu have culture. Modern humans have been around for over 1,500,000 years or more, originating here in Afraka as all other stages did, and they all had cultures.

"When you begin to document civilizations, you are documenting, one, written language; two, sophisticatedly planned architectural structures; three, planned cities—not just villages; four, a functional calendar and organization of time and space; five, an organized economy with planned agriculture and animal domestication; and six, a defense force or military to defend and protect your civilization from barbarians and savages. Only ancient Kash met these criteria one thousand years after the last great flood. Afrakan Kmt met these criteria almost two thousand years later. And there was nothing civilized in ancient Asia until we came there almost two thousand years ago. The Annunaki did not bring civilization to your world. They enslaved you and used the people as slaves to mine gold. There have been other intelligent live beings who have come and gone, but none of them gave you civilization. Only we, the Annu, through the Medjay warriors and scientists, brought civilization to you.

"Humans have built and destroyed many advanced civilizations on this planet. The same process is being repeated as we speak. We are standing at the doorstep of a new coming of civilization in the world under the leadership of the second golden age after the great flood in Kemet. Chief Medjay Jhutyms Ka-en-Heru, he witnessed the birth of your great-grandfather and trained your great-grandfather as a Medjay," said the Hem Ntchr Tepy Medjay Hu-Sia.

"He was there at the birth of your grandfather and your grandfather's children's birth. That includes your father's birth and your birth. And the chief Medjay named you because he said you had your great- grandfather's soul and the power to reunite ancient Kemet into one nation again."

Medjay Hu-Sia stood up as he faced the crown prince. "You do not have to know where your vision is taking you. You simply have to trust where your vision is taking you. Your vision is not a mistake. The mistake is not following it. The mistake is not trusting it. The mistake is not surrendering to that which flows from the Divine Spirit."

"Where is the Divine Spirit?" I said.

"It is not in the world, which is an illusion. It's in your mind," he replied. "Become aware of all your thoughts in terms of polarity and vibratory quality. Let your higher consciousness guard your doorway of thought. Carefully supervise and cultivate your thought life."

He paused as he stared into the crown prince's eye.

"The chief Medjay said his fifth Shemsu Heru would be a priest scientist that would unite Upper and Lower Kemet once again. Each human being is born into this life with a certain mission and with certain seeds or tools that are the products of past lives, endeavors, and experiences. The chief Medjay Jhutyms Ka-en-Heru is never wrong. He is a Djedi, a great divine seer. That's why you are here, great royal crown prince Mentchu-hotep, because you are to become the fifth Shemsu Heru." And then he dropped down on one knee and bowed his head before me with tears in his eyes.

CHAPTER 6

TA NTCHR, THE LAND OF DIVINITY

During the next year and a half, I traveled as a Medjay with my unit of Medjay medju to the mountains of the moon at Mount Choke and Lake Tana, the source of the western Hapy Eteru (Blue Nile). The Abbai portion of the Blue Nile rises at Lake Tana and flows for nineteen miles (thirty kilometers) before plunging over the Tis Issat Falls, "smoking water" in Amharic. The river then loops across northwest Kash (Ethiopia) through a series of deep valleys and canyons into Meroe. There, it is known only as the Blue Nile, Hapy Eteru.

The Blue Nile is a river originating in Ethiopia, ancient Kash. With the White Nile, the river is one of the two major tributaries of the Hapy Eteru (Nile). The upper reaches of the river are called the Abbai in Ethiopia, where it is still sacred in the same exact way that it was sacred during ancient Kemet (ancient Egypt). It is so beautiful and still brings fresh soil down the Hapy Eteru (Nile) to lower Kemet (Egypt).

At the great Tis Issat Falls that flows from Lake Tana, the mouth of the mountain of the moon, we the Medjay medju all dove in with no fear from forty meters into the rushing water, and no one was injured. It is said by the local villagers that only a Medjay warrior can do this and live.

The Blue Nile, originating in breathtaking natural springs above Lake Tana in Mt. Choqa, which is in the northwestern part of Kash, has been untouched by time for thousands of years. The river has played a significant role in human ourstory by supplying the majority of the water for the Hapy Eteru, providing the means for the land through which it flowed to be agriculturally productive. Having the Hapy's floodwaters to depend on gave rise to stable early human settlements and the Kemet civilization. From there, we took the trade routes to Ymnsqt, the Red sea, and travelled up the east coast to Punt or Pwenet. We escorted several different trade groups who paid us well for their security. Here we hunted in the high country for mushrooms and healing plants and followed the tracks of Ta-Sety hunters and the Twa who were there thousands of years before them. I entered into hidden places and listened to their song. There are riches here that make gold pale in their light, Mrr that is larger than the moon, a way of life that is a mode of being, and a multidimensionality of experiences that makes a good book a shadow. There is a spirit here that invites you to enter it. But it is not an easy thing to do even though it is the most natural. It is *the way* and *the way is Ma'at.*

Punt indeed seems to have been a commercial center for goods not only from within its own borders, but also from elsewhere in Ta Ntchr. The land of Punt was sacred to the Kemetyu of Kemet as one of the sources of their race. Here the Kemetyu of Kemet sought and found many items that did not exist within the two lands in Kemet or Kash. From Punt, they received the incense known as *antyu,* also frankincense and myrrh, which was produced in considerable quantities near Punt in the region of Utjenet (Ntchru Land) or Ta Ntchr, as well as ivory, gold, iron ores, precious stones, ebony (hebny), and gum (Kemy). From this mystical place, they also imported the skins of giraffes, panthers, and cheetahs, which were worn by temple priests, priestess, and sometimes the live animals themselves for their own amusement or spiritual purposes. For example, the sacred cynocephalus baboons were imported from Punt. Because of the goods from Punt used by priest and priestess and to adorn temples, it was known as a region of Ntchru land and considered a personal pleasure garden of the Ntchr Amen and Khnum. The land of Punt, with its reed beehive-shaped houses rising on stilts above water, was the most exotic and mysterious of places to visit. I enjoyed the semiprecious and precious gemstones the most. In Kemet, we had malachite, turquoise, jasper, amethyst, carnelian, alabaster, and quartzite. But here I saw diamonds, clear quartz, smoky quartz, pyrite, ruby, garnet, onyx, citrine, bloodstone, obsidian, moonstones, rose quartz, agates, howlite, tiger's eye, emeralds, and my favorite lapis lazuli along with dozens of other exotic stones I had never seen or heard of before. I purchased every beautiful gemstone I could get my hands on in threes and sent them back to Kemet to my mother and sister, Neferu. The records will show that several voyages of the royalty of Punt came to the court of the Nswt Bety in Kash and Kemet. And the royal Punt family, they were always escorted by the famous Medjay warriors. Our last day in Punt is permanently etched in my mind forever. The Nswt Mwt Ntchrt wrt (the great royal mother of the Ntchru at Punt) is part of the immortal Psdju. She is not only a Medjay, but she is a Djedi and the second daughter of the chief Medjay Jhutyms Ka-en-Heru. She allowed her female Medjay warriors to perform for us. I had heard about the legendary female Medjay warriors, but I had never met any or seen them in action.

Female Medjay warriors

I know that Medjay Ka-en-Jhutyms from Barwat and Medjay Akhtoy Ba-Heru from Punt and even the Hem Sem Tepy of Amen-Ra, Medjay Hu-Sia, all have Medjay warrior mothers. I heard they are mostly employed as bodyguards to the royal mothers and royal wives. That evening, more than fifty Medjay women performed for us, and I was in complete amazement. Their forms were impeccable. They used softer but very efficient movements, almost dance-like, and they used much lighter weapons but just as deadly. They had flying darts used as hairpins and clothespins, and they had excellent bowmanship, were great in close dagger attacks, and had extremely impressive spear- and swordplay. Each one was strikingly beautiful. I had never seen such beauty gathered in one area before in my life. Just their beauty alone was a weapon. To close the demonstration, one of the Medjay women warriors fought two Asiatic swordsmen almost twice her size, and she defeated both of them with ease with her longsword play.

Later Medjay Bennu told me that she was Medjay Akhtoy's mother and the second wife of the chief Medjay Jhutyms Ka-en-Heru. I smiled to myself, thinking, *When I'm the Shemsu Heru, I need at least two or three of these divine women in my royal palace.* When we think of the divine, thoughts of light, love, beauty, patience, understanding, and compassion bathe our mind and consciousness.

Then we traveled on land by foot and by boat along the spice trails of east Afraka. Most of the gold and silver and useful metals we accumulated along the way, we gave away to poor villagers and the common hardworking people. The gemstones, I sent to my mother and sister.

We traveled until the beaches met the bushes at Kilwa, a large trading post on the east Afrakan coast. Here palm trees sway in the cooling ocean breeze. White sand and blue waters sparkled, alluring beneath the tropical sun, Ra. You could see dhows drift past, propelled by billowing white sails, while Swahili fishermen cast their nets below a brilliant red sunset.

The animal life we encountered as we walked inland toward Kilimanjaro included giraffes, buffalo, warthogs, common waterbucks, reedbucks, hartebeest, wildebeest, red duikers, greater kudu, sable antelopes, yellow baboon, and vervet monkeys. We saw herds of up to thirty elephants and several lion prides. My father loved hunting for big cats, and his favorite robe was made of lion skin that he caught himself.

We saw leopards, spotted hyenas, and black-backed jackals, and out of all of these creatures, I only hated the hyenas. I mean I really disliked those scavengers. They reminded me of the lowly pale Asian scavengers of the north who plundered the dead and who stole sacred offerings at night and who had no respect for women. Medjay Ka-en-Jhutyms told me several times I needed to forgive them and release that energy into the universe. I'm still working on that. As we traveled by boat, we encountered hippos that grunted disapprovingly in the distance and monstrous crocodiles, invisible except for a pair of sentry-post eyes that peeked menacingly above the surface. We saw plenty of marine and riverine birds including the flamingos, the cranes, the goliath herons, the fish eagles, and the great falcons, which were so respected in Kemet and Kash because of their hunting skills and mastery of their domain. During my first trip to Kilimanjaro, I managed to miss most of this beauty because of all the pain I was encountering. Now I can see with my new eyes that Kilimanjaro epitomizes the beauty of east Afraka, Ta Ntchr. Its legendary snowcapped dome, atop a perfectly formed extinct volcano, stands at the summit of Ta Ntchr, 5,895 meters or 19,336 feet

above sea level. More significantly, as viewed from its base, this is the world's tallest freestanding mountain, rising in breathtaking isolation to tower an imperious five kilometers or three miles above the surrounding savannah.

We journeyed to the top in three days, taking on the challenge. We traveled high, to the heights of the earth, to seek the wisdom that only mountains know. We followed the path set before us, our bodies adapting itself to the rhythms of the land, to the rise and fall of the soul. Through relentless struggle, we came to the top, a place where we could see the soul of the earth before us, and we could feel the vast mountain spirit all around us.

We trained hard, meditated, and slept our first day. Here I learned of the two types of stamina. I was always conscious of physical stamina, but spiritual stamina is developed as our spiritual energies flow through the psychic nature and by means of service. Stamina is the reward of Ma'at. At the top of the world on Kilimanjaro, we sat in a circle to meditate together. As my body began to relax and breathe, I noticed all anxieties, fears, and worries slowly disappeared as peace flooded my entire being—body, mind, and soul. I lost myself in the beauty of the nonexistence of time and space. I seem to be sitting in midair, maybe ten feet above my body, as I heard Medjay Ka-en-Jhutyms speak, but his voice was coming from the clouds.

"This peace is the very essence of your being. Your soul is dispensing this peace upon every section and function of your mind and body. This condition and place of peace is always available to you. Know this and use it at any time. It is never separated from you as the Divine Spirit is never separated from you. You need no longer feel afraid, alone, or disturbed. You are secured and protected. The power of the infinite is now flowing to and through you."

This was the joy and peace that the chief Medjay Jhutyms Ka-en- Heru had felt when we were here last. Now I know that some degree of enlightenment is necessary before this connection can be recognized. Until light is reflected into the human consciousness, the intellectual brain cannot make a conscious connection to the real self, the spiritual self, and to its purpose and goal.

Later the second day, we sat and nestled ourselves into meditation positions, and I began to breathe deeply, to relax, to let myself drop down and to be held by this place. I opened my feelings wide, and let the field of my heart range out far beyond me. I could feel Geb making contact with Nut as she towered over me. I let myself be filled with the power of the mountain. I could feel the awesome presence of Kilimanjaro all around me. I breathed it in, letting it touch and fill me. I felt a presence that was older than any animal or any *remtch*. My heart was in contact with an awareness that is far beyond me as the stars are from Ra.

Nature gave me all that I have ever wanted to have and began to teach me a truth that I had not learned in the temples, a truth plain in its every line and movement and truth that is beyond the remtch for nature does not know how to lie. In nature's presence, we are all children, nothing more. And all our honors, titles, and even riches lose their significance and importance in its majesty. After two great days on top of the world, we began our descent also in two days, going through Medjay training drills as we descended back from this earthly heaven. Now I can understand the heavenly look on Medjay Jhutyms Ka-en-Heru's face when we were here a little more than four years ago when he said to me, "There are many paths to the top of the mountain, but the view is always the same."

By now, my animal fighting skills had caught the attentions of my seniors, and Medjay Sia-en-hotep asked me for the first time in two years to teach my two cat forms, Simba, the lion, and *paka weusi*, the black panther, which were taught to me by the chief of all Medjay, Jhutyms Ka-en-Heru, to three of the five new Medjay in our group. Medjay Ipi of Napata and Medjay Akhtoy had already learned these forms with Medjay Ka-en-Jhutyms from the chief Medjay Jhutyms Ka-en-Heru himself. This also was one of my high points, and I finally felt like I was contributing to the unit.

We were now walking across the great Serengeti savannas of Ta Ntchr, one of my favorite places and one of the most beautiful sights on earth. We will follow the great migration of millions of animals as they take their annual exodus north, covering over one million kilometers or six hundred miles. If you are a cat lover like most of the Medjay in our group, then this was like heaven on earth because we got a chance to really see them, the great cats in action. The spectacle of predator versus prey dominates here in the savanna. Golden-manned lions feast on an abundance of plain grazers. Solitary leopards haunt acacia trees along the river while lightning-fast cheetahs prowl the open plains. In Kemet, the black jackal is called Enpu or Anpu, and he is the guide dog to resurrection and rebirth. Here in the Serengeti, all three Afrakan jackal species live and hunt alongside the spotted hyena and a host of more elusive small predators from the insectivorous aardwolf to the beautiful serval cat. Each day after observing a kill or an evasive move, we would gather around and teach each other what we saw, especially if that could be used in our Medjay training.

Being here right now with these Medjay warriors is worth all their weight together in gold to me, I thought. We were developing a bond that would link and tie us closely together for the rest of our physical lives.

There was more to the Serengeti than large mammals. There were also wooded hills and towering termite mounds that looked like pyramid builders. There were rivers infested with crocodiles but also lined with fig trees and acacia woodland stained orange by dust. Gaudy agama lizards and rock hyraxes scuffled around isolated granite kopjes. The dung beetle is called Kheper and represent coming into being, a form of transformation. Well, here you could see more than one hundred varieties of dung beetles and five hundred plus bird species. Surely, I thought this had to be the closest thing to paradise or the original garden of humans. This was why we called our total land Ta Khenset, the land of the placenta or the land of our birthplace on earth.

Above all this beauty was the liberating sense of space that characterized the sunburnt plains as it stretched into a shimmering golden horizon at the end of the earth. After the rains, this golden grassy expanse was transformed into a lush green carpet flecked with wildflowers. Colors became more vivid, and the air began to sparkle. My breathing and the sounds of the savanna took on a luminous quality.

It was here while reflecting on all that the chief Medjay had taught me that I realized that my eyes and ears had changed again. Even when the Medjay had downtime, I found myself practicing every form, every posture, every stance meticulously, reviewing my animals, and studying the Ntchru. My knowledge of plants and herbs were rivaling even my senior Medjay warriors, and they were all very impressed with my progress. My sight was keener, and my ears were sharper than ever before, but nevertheless, I heard no sounds other than those I had already heard. I paid strict attention to my diet, eating only once a day and fasting monthly. Then one morning as I was sitting under a large baobab tree in one of my meditation postures from Ma'at Akhw Ba Ankh, I started to discern faint sounds unlike those I had ever heard before. The more acutely I listened, the clearer the sounds became. The feeling of enlightenment enveloped me. *These must be the sounds that the chief Medjay Jhutyms Ka-en-Heru and the Hem Ntchr Tepy of Kemet wished for me to discern*, I thought.

My heart was bursting with joy. I wanted to rush to the Medjay Ka-en-Jhutyms and tell him all that I heard and saw. It took all my Medjay training to disguise my feelings. We entered the great Ngoro Ngoro Crater, the world's largest unbroken caldera. Even here, we encountered elephants, lions, cheetahs, wildebeests, buffalos, and the black rhinos. Once again I witnessed beauty that I thought could not be matched, and that evening, tears clouded my eyes as I thought how honored I was to witness these great wonders of our world. Finally, that evening in private, I asked to speak to Medjay Ka-en-Jhutyms, and he agreed. We walked along the tall grasses of the great Ngoro Ngoro Crater. I explained to him what I had heard, felt, and seen over the last week. Medjay Ka-en-Jhutyms was very calm and poised like his father, and it was amazing because he was so young, just a few years older than myself, but light years ahead of me in experience and ability. He explained to me what was happening for it had happened to him the same way.

He spoke with great wisdom, "Hearing means accurate perception, and when accurate perception becomes a habit, then hearing well leads to speaking well. When your actions are guided by good speech, this is called Mdw Nefer. As a result of accurate perception, an unconscious mastery fills the body from the Divine Spirit world of all knowing."

He said his father had told him what to do when this moment came. "When you open the spiritual door of your intuition, you must trust everything you receive. The ancestors and the spirit world speak through your intuition. Trust it. It's there for a reason. It will lead you to places and resources beyond your imagination."

He gave me a blue pouch with crushed mushrooms in it and explained what I was to do and to meet him after they ate that night.

That night after dinner, around a blazing campfire, Medjay Ka-en- Jhutyms explained to our Medjay medju that it was time to return to Kemet. Our mission was at the 90 percent level, and the last 10 percent was to visit the Ruwenzori Mountains, the source of Hapy Eteru Reshy, and return safely with all of us in excellent condition to Kemet as one Medjay medju. All the Medjay spoke as one voice.

"Dwa Ntchr Amen-Ra Mentchu!"

"We have all grown this last two years mentally, physically, and spiritually. The key to spiritual growth is to be open and to stay open. Liberate your mind and soul by going wherever you feel you must go for your own growth, even if you think you're alone because others may not understand or understand. The task is not to bring you in alignment with the expectations of others but to align yourself with the Divine Spirit. Then your soul and the great ancestors who are your appointed guides can lead you home to heaven. So with that in your consciousness, tonight we dance and drum," spoke Medjay Ka-en-Jhutyms.

"Part of the reason you are excelling so well in this illusion is because you've had many spiritual experiences in other lifetimes, Prince Mentchu-hotep. This is also why you will also take too many of these ideas and lessons like a duck takes to water. Your combined lifetimes of learning are still within your mind, and your enlightenment is just a state of remembering."

As we positioned ourselves around the campfire, Medjay Ka-en- Jhutyms spoke again. "In the Medjay and Kashite culture, the drum is a transportation device that carries the listener into other worlds. Only the sound of the drum has the power to make one travel in this specific way. Where the sound ship goes, everybody goes. To refuse to drum is to refuse to travel. To forget how to drum is to forget how to feel. Let's drum, Medjay warriors, let's drum!"

I ate the mushrooms and began to play with them. I was playing really well I mean, like a real master drummer—and I was just getting into it when my drum vanished in thin air. But none of the other Medjay noticed a thing, and they continued to play like master drummers. As their drums began to beat faster and faster, my whole body rose up off the ground, and I began spinning around the fire, dancing over the flames in perfect harmony with their drumbeats. Gravity was no longer in control of me, but I was in control of all the elements around me. The fire was not hot even though its flames were blazing three feet high. Yes, this was an illusion, and I was having a dream within a dream.

I could see through my flesh. I had become some kind of light being as I began to glow. Part of my spirit flew right out of my head into space, traveling faster than light, penetrating planets and stars like air. I was swirling around the galaxy like a giant star, and then I exploded like a supernova into billions of pieces. But all of what had become of me was sucked into a black hole, and there was nothingness and silence.

After a great silence, I emerged as a black cat. No, I was still transforming, and I was a huge black panther. I walked softly because I could smell the humans one hundred meters away as I peered through the tall savanna grasses. There was a hunting party of Maasai warriors. I charged out at them. There must have been ten of them, and they threw their spears and clubs at me. But I ate their weapons, and then I ate them all one by one. They could not escape. I was so swift that I was untouched, and when there was only one Maasai still standing, their leader, I could feel his fear as sweat beaded down his face beside his long hair. He pissed himself with fright, and then with my mighty paw, I smacked him to the ground, leaving a nasty claw mark across his chest. And I could smell him defecating all over himself, bleeding from the blades of my claws and trembling uncontrollably with his eyes closed. I roared almost like a lion as he passed out. Then I walked away slowly back into the tall savanna grasses. I left him there to live and to remember me for the rest of his life.

The next morning, I awakened very slowly, just keeping my eye closed for a moment or two. I could hear my own heartbeat and feel my blood flowing through my veins like Hapy. I could hear and feel the movements of every Medjay in our group with my new hearing. But as sharp as my new hearing was, I could not hear Medjay Ka-en-Jhutyms, Medjay Akhtoy Ba-Heru, or Medjay Ipi.

Were they here? I thought. I opened my eyes slowly, and I could see all nine of the Medjay.

Hmmm, I wondered, *why could I not hear them? They are surely their father's children,* I thought. *But how about Medjay Ipi, who is he?*

There was a large bowl of water at my side, and I knew Medjay Ka- en-Jhutyms had placed it there. As I looked down at my hands, they were filled with blood. I wondered if anyone else saw them. I quickly placed them in the water and scrubbed them well, and then I got a glance of my reflection in the water. I jumped back quickly, knocking the bowl over. I had seen the reflection of a black panther in the bowl.

Medjay Bennu Henenu picked up the bowl as he asked me, "Is everything all right, Prince Mentchu-hotep?"

While he was looking at me strangely, I touched my face with my hands, but it felt normal. Medjay Ka-en-Jhutyms had poured his magic herb powder into some water and told me to drink this, and everything would be fine.

About an hour later, Medjay Ka-en-Jhutyms asked me how I feel. "I felt stronger than ever," I told him.

"I saw everything," he said, "and it's all right. Matter appears out of nowhere, but what is less obvious and yet necessary to realize is that after it appears, it is still nowhere. All space is empty and nonexistent, even the tiny fraction of it that appears to contain something."

He placed his hand on my shoulder as he spoke, "Deep in the human unconscious mind is a pervasive need for a logical universe that makes sense. But in reality, the universe is an illusion that is always one step beyond logic. If you believe the universe exists, you cannot escape or get out of the universe. The universe is a scenario. As long as you believe the illusion, its laws always define you. As Medjay warriors, we can bend or step out of the illusion through the power of Divine spirit." We were only two-hour run away from the mouth of the Hapy

Eteru Reshy where there was a Medjay temple and trading camp.

Medjay Ka-en-Jhutyms explained, "We might encounter Maasai warriors because we have to travel through their territory in order to save time. The alternative route is around the mountains, and that would take a day or two. I speak their language, so if we encounter them, leave all the talking to me. They might try and challenge us. We fought against them about one hundred years ago over the land where our Medjay camp is now standing. They suffered a terrible defeat, losing thousands of warriors. They are very stubborn and would not surrender or accept defeat even though they were no match against Chief Medjay Jhutyms Ka-en-Heru's elite Medjay warriors."

Maasai warriors of east Afraka

Chief Medjay Jhutyms Ka-en-Heru had already educated me on the history of the warrior clans here in Ta Ntchr Resewt, including the Maasai, the Samburu, and the Kalenjin. They were pastoralists, but they were also famous for their fearsome reputations as warriors and cattle rustlers. According to their own oral ourstory, the Maasai originated from the lower Hapy, Hapy Valley north of Lake Turkana. Their main weapons were the spears and shields, but they were most feared for throwing clubs (*orinka*), which could be accurately thrown from up to seventy paces (about one hundred meters). All of the Medjay medju was aware of their history but most of us had never encountered them. We were making excellent time, about thirty minutes into our run, when we encountered a small group of about twenty Maasai warriors on patrol. They flagged us down, and their leader seemed very angry.

Medjay Ka-en-Jhutyms gave his spear to Medjay Sia-hotep and said "I'll handle this" as he walked straight up to their leader. Words were exchanged. Their leader pointed in the direction of the mountains, indicating that that was the way we need to be traveling and that we needed special permission to travel through their territory. Medjay Ka- en-Jhutyms basically told their leader in a calm but strong voice that Medjay warriors don't need permission to travel any place in the land of Ntchr. The Maasai warriors all jumped into combat formation, and so did we.

Medjay Ka-en-Jhutyms waved us down, then he spoke again to their leader, "No one needs to die here. You are not our match."

Their leader smiled. "Are you blind? We outnumber you twenty to ten."

"No, I see very well, and the odds is about one hundred to twenty, in our favor with no way for you to win." replied Medjay Ka-en-Jhutyms. "You must be tired of living," the Maasai leader said to Medjay Ka-en-Jhutyms.

"Who are your most powerful warriors here? I shall take five of them, and I will use no weapon," replied Medjay Ka-en-Jhutyms. "And then you will understand."

The Maasai leader smiled as he pointed to five of his warriors.

"This ought to be easy," their leader replied to his Maasai warriors who were all about six feet six. They quickly encircled their Medjay opponent. I looked over at Medjay Sia-hotep. He had a smile on his face, and so did the other Medjay. In fact, they relaxed their spears and shields as they watched. All five of the Maasai warriors lunged their spears at Medjay Ka-en-Jhutyms at one time. The Medjay dropped very low under their attack and swept three off their feet with a single circular sweep. And then he leaped into the other two before they could regain their balance, breaking one spear in half and ripping the spear out of the other's hand as his wheel kick landed hard on the Maasai's head, smashing him unconscious to the ground. Medjay Ka-en-Jhutyms took the Maasai spear and smashed the three Maasai who were trying to recover from the Medjay's powerful sweep with two blows, knocking out two of the Maasai and kicking the third on the side of his head, rendering him also unconscious.

All five Maasai lay on the ground, four out cold and the fifth holding his ankle like it was broken. The other Maasai looked on in disbelief at their fallen comrades. Medjay Ka-en-Jhutyms then took the Maasai spear and threw it toward the Maasai village. Their mouths dropped open wide when the spear actually flew out of sight. Medjay Ka-en-Jhutyms than grabbed their leaders spear out of his hand and threw it in the same direction, and it traveled completely out of sight also. Medjay Ka-en-Jhutyms grabbed the leader by his arm and then turned quickly and just pointed his finger at the other Maasai, telling them not to move if they wanted him to live.

Medjay Ka-en-Jhutyms said to their leader, "Look into my eyes." He pulled him closer. The Maasai leader could see a huge black panther in the Medjay's eyes, walking slowly through tall grasses.

The black panther in their vision

He could see a hunting party of Maasai warriors in which he, the viewer, was leading. The black panther charged out at them, and there must have been ten of them. They threw their spears and clubs at the black panther, but it ate their weapons and then ate them all one by one. And because the black panther was so swift it was untouched. There was only the Maasai leader standing. He could feel his own fear as sweat beaded off his face down the side of his long hair. He pissed himself with fright, and then the huge black panther took its mighty paw and smacked him to the ground, leaving a nasty claw mark across his chest. He smelled from his own defecation running down his legs and all over himself, bleeding from the deep cuts from the panther's claws, trembling uncontrollable with his eyes closed. Then he heard the black panther roar like a lion as he passed out. At that very moment, the Maasai leader fell to the ground in a pool of his own piss and feces, and the other Maasai warriors who could move, ran to his side.

"Look at his chest. Are those panther or lion claw marks?"

"We have to stop the bleeding," one Maasai cried out as they held their noses from the stench. The Maasai warriors had their hands full, caring for their leader and the still stunned and wounded Maasai warriors still lying on the ground. In the midst of all that commotion and confusion, Medjay Ka-en-Jhutyms walked back over to us, picked up his spear, and closed his eyes for a moment as if in prayer.

"You will come to know and experience that the Ntchr is never outside of you. When you realize this fact, you will no longer identify yourself with a vulnerable body. You will learn instead of your true reality as pure spirit that is invulnerable forever. I forgive their ignorance, and I forgive myself. Let's go, we have a boat to catch."

We arrived at the Medjay camp at noon just like Medjay Ka-en- Jhutyms had planned. Medjay Sia-en-hotep told all of us that food would be ready in twenty minutes and to wash and get ready.

While we were eating, Medjay Ni-Sobek sat next to me and asked, "Have you ever seen anyone throw a spear like that before?" I told him that I had seen Chief Medjay Jhutyms Ka-en-Heru, his father, do the same feat.

"The best is yet to come," I told Medjay Ni-Sobek. "What do you mean?" he said.

"When the Maasai get home, they're going to find both spearheads stuck in one hole that they can't pull out."

"Wow, I would love to see their faces after that." Ni-Sobek smiled. Back at the Maasai village, one of the Maasai warriors found their spears stuck in a single hole in a large baobab tree at the center of their village.

"Come, help me pull my spear out," he said to one of his comrades. But they could not budge the spears. By now, there was a large group of Maasai who had circled the spears. Four or five Maasai warriors tried to pull the spears out of the tree, but they could not budge it. The Maasai chief heard all the commotion and asked how the spears had gotten there. When the Maasai warriors told the chief what had happened and about their encounter with the Medjay warriors, the chief was quiet for a moment and then called for a village meeting of all the Maasai in their village—men, women, and children.

The high priest of the village spoke first, and after libation was poured, he introduced the chief.

The Maasai chief said, "I want our great elder to speak to you because he was there when we fought against the Medjay warriors one hundred years ago."

The great elder stood up with the help of his staff and looked into the eyes of his Maasai family.

"I must say we are great warriors, and we have never met our match among men. But the Medjay warriors are not ordinary men. Their origins are not from this earth, and their leaders are operating with a superior intellect with great inner spiritual powers. They are warriors from another time and dimension that came here to bring balance to the earth by fighting the beast who lives underground. When the Maasai had a dispute with the Medjay over some land, they tried to warn us, but our arrogance got in the way. We went to war. We gathered our neighboring kinsmen and went into full battle. We outnumbered them by the thousands. We had gathered maybe five thousand Maasai warriors against maybe one hundred Medjay warriors.

"The Medjay chief tried to talk to us, but we would not listen. We thought they were scared and were begging for mercy. We sent our first wave of one thousand Maasai warriors at them, thinking that that would be enough. The Medjay formed three circles, one inside another. In the protected inner circle were bowmen, and they picked us off like flies with their arrows that never missed. The second circle were swordsmen, who chopped us up like cattle, and their outer wall with shields and swords and shields and spears alternating were their elite Medjay warriors. And within sixty minutes of fighting, there were no Maasai standing. We were in shock.

"Their chief, Medjay Jhutyms Ka-en-Heru, I could still see his powerful golden-brown structure glistening in the sun, tried to communicate with our chief again to stop this unnecessary madness of a massacre. But our chief was so furious that he sent three thousand Maasai into battle, knowing that would finish the Medjay off. The Medjay changed their formation into some kind of six-pointed star formation, two pyramids facing two directions. Our Maasai warriors just got into each other's way. It was a mess, and limbs and Maasai heads were flying everywhere. They had superior weapons, superior skills, superior strength, and superior war technology.

After we lost about two thousand more Maasai warriors, we retreated, literally destroyed, and psychologically devastated. Our warriors threw down their weapons and begged and cried for mercy like babies. Their chief asked only to speak with our chiefs, but all our chiefs were all killed in battle. So the chief Medjay spoke with our only living high priest and queen mother and offered to help bury our dead and restore order, but they, the Medjay, were going to build a Medjay camp on the Hapy Eteru ten miles away. And they hoped there will never be a problem between them again. Our high priest and queen mother agreed. They signed the treaty with Maasai blood.

"The Medjay warriors stayed for three days, restoring Ma'at. They helped the wounded and sick and buried and burned the dead. They were the bravest yet kindest of men and for the next year helped retrain our warriors as they built a magnificent temple near the bank of the Hapy Eteru hdjet, White Nile. We, the elders, apologize to the young Maasai warriors who challenged these mighty Medjay warriors for you did not know what you were up against and you acted in the same arrogant manner as your forefathers.

"So listen carefully, Maasai, now you know. They, the Medjay, are our protectors. They could have killed you all in the blink of an eye, but instead they chose the road of peace but not without teaching you a small lesson. So in the future, whenever you see them, drop on one knee and bow your head with great respect. I hope this is understood. Those unmovable spears at the center of our village, let them stay because they represent a sign of the Medjay warriors' awesome powers."

I took a deep breath, knowing this might be my last trip this far south again. Medjay Sia-en-hotep just briefed us that battle had started again over the borders of Upper and Lower Kemet. I walked alone along the shore for a moment and then looked back near our campsite and marveled at its beauty. I see why the Medjay chose this land, and I could see also why the Maasai fought to keep it. This was a tropical floral paradise, as my new eyes scanned the view of a multitude of orchids, stunning yellow-orange redhot pokers, and a variety of aloes, proteas, geraniums, giant lobelias, lilies, and aster daisies. The local people here call it Bustani ya mungu—garden of the Creator. My eyes quickly caught a glance of a colony of blue swallow. In Kemet, this bird image repesented the symbol of great or greatness. As I walked back to join my Medjay comrades, butterflies danced around me. I saw a chameleon, a lizard, and a frog, all enhancing the biological wealth of Bustani ya mungu.

When I looked up, Medjay Ka-en-Jhutyms was standing next to me, smiling. He just apeared out of thin air.

I asked him, "What happened to the Maasai warrior when he looked into your eyes?"

"The world of the Medjay does not distinguish between reality and imagination. To us, there is a close connection between thought and reality. To imagine something, to closely focus one's thought on it has the potential to bring that something into being. Those who take a tragic view of life and are always expecting the worst usually manifest that reality. Those who expect that things will work out for the best usually experience just that. Let's just say he went on a magical journey with a huge black panther, and he will never forget it.

"Anger is never justified. Attacking has no foundation, and fear imprisons you, so there is no escape. Listen carefully, there can be meaning that is nonverbal. There cannot be meaning that is nonlinguistic for the same reason that there cannot be a triangle that is not three- sided." He did it again, messing with my head. Now I'll be thinking about this all week.

We walked slowely through the beautiful Medjay temple, which was dedicated to Khnum, admiring the Mdw Ntchr perfectly inscribed on the walls and columns. This temple looked like it was in Kemet, the same great archecture aligned with the stars. So above, so below.

"This is the work of Priest Tut-ankh-Ra of Napata," Medjay Ka- en-Jhutyms said as he placed his hand on my shoulder. I knew I would miss all these. I took a deep breath as I inhaled the fresh air as well as the breathtaking scenery. The royal Medjay boat was packed and ready to go. We would be using the sails this time as we travel down north with the current and the winds with us. This royal Medjay boat was the winged cobra.

Hapy Eteru flowing through Ta Ntchr

CHAPTER 7

MY FIRST TEST AS A MEDJAY WARRIOR

As our royal cobra boat sailed away from the sacred Temple of Khnum in Ta Ntchr, my eyes were drunk from this magnificent scenery. I knew this would be my last visit to this very sacred place. So I sipped the view slowly as Shu, the southern breeze, guided our royal vessel northward toward Ruwenzori Mountains and the source of Hapy Eteru Reshy. The atmosphere was very different now, and we were going to war. Medjay Sia-en-hotep was the first to break the long silence.

"Your Medjay ancestors have your back. Know that you're not alone no matter what you're going through. And know that your journey and challenges are not mistakes but tests to bring out the best of your character. Allow them to speak through your heart, intellect, and inspiration. Be still and sense their presence all around you, knowing that all is in divine order. We must move forward now without any trace of doubt or fear, lest you place an illusion of an obstacle in your way. The quality of your thoughts determines the quality of your experiences. Think victorious even before the battle has started. May our sacred and great Medjay ancestors bless us above and beyond your most heavenly imagination."

Every Medjay was even more focused, our weapons ready and our ears fine-tuned for any unusual sound that might be danger. Medjay Ni- Sobek and Medjay Bennu Henenu had first watch detail with their bows and arrows in their hands. They both could shoot flies at fifty meters, and their bow skills were impecable. I have never felt safer in my life as I looked into the eyes and faces of each of these warriors. The two leaders, Medjay Ka-en-Jhutyms and Medjay Sia-en-hotep, both men were part of the chief Medjay Jhutyms Ka-en-Heru elite Medjay unit, undefeated in over twenty battles between them. Medjay Ka-en-Jhutyms is Kash's ten times all around national champion.

The last five Medjay fitted in so well with our group, and it was like we were always together. I looked at them one by one. Medjay Khety was our *sesh* (scribe) and *sdjawty* (treasurer), and he recorded the journey and kept records of supplies and equipment. What an incredible memory he had besides being an incredible swordsman. He was taught personally by Chief Medjay Jhutyms Ka-en-Heru.

Next was Medjay Meket-Ra. He was the youngest next to myself. Even though he was only twenty, he was a three-time Nuba wrestling champion with incredible strength. I've seen him lift boulders that four strong men could not budge. It is said if he can touch you, you are defeated, and if he grabs you, you're an ancestor.

Next was Medjay Akhtoy Ba-Heru. He is from Punt and is also the son of the chief Medjay Jhutyms Ka-en-Heru. Medjay Ka-en-Jhutyms is his senior, and their mothers are sisters. I was informed by Medjay Bennu Henenu that his skills are only second to Medjay Ka-en-Jhutyms on this team, and he was a five-time all around Mentchu combat champion in Punt and the junior of Medjay Ka-en-jhutyms by three years.

Next there was Medjay Ka-en-Heru-Bes from Ta Bes, the extreme south and the land of the great trees. He traveled the farthest. And next to Medjay Ka-en-Jhutyms is the only warrior on this team that has master's rank in ten different weapons. His father is one of the immortal Psdju, and he is a Djedi of the south.

All the Medjay except me have master's rank in at least five weapons—the bow and arrow, the spear and long pole, sword, dagger, and short sticks. I was still working on my short stick tecniques. I had seen Medjay Ka-en-Heru Bes shoot flies out the air with his blowing bamboo reed. He also is a master of the throwing sticks, chain and sickle, throwing knives, stars and darts, and some secret object in his shoulder holster called a slingshot. Medjay Ka-en-Heru Bes is also our booby trap expert. If it moves, he can trap it.

Last but not least is Medjay Ipi. He was the Hm Sem Tepy of the temple of Heru in Napata and is the older brother of Prince Piye and Princesses Tem and Kawit. He, like Medjay Ka-en-Jhutyms and Medjay Akhtoy Ba-Heru, has mastered the seven animals and five elements of the Medjay combat system. I've heard Medjay Benu Henenu and Medjay Ni-Sobek mention that many Medjay still talk about Medjay Ipi's two-hour battle with Medjay Hu-Sia, the Hm Sem Tepy of Amen-Ra at Barwat. The judges stopped the battle and declared both of them twin champions of Napata three years ago. There is such a bond here that we can finish each other's sentences because we are Medjay medju, one unit.

The Ruwenzori Mountains of Ta Ntchr

When I looked up, I was face to face with the famous Ruwenzori Mountains of the moon. Medjay Ipi pointed out that "the Ruwenzori are the only high mountains of Ta Khenset that were not created by volcanic activity. The name Ruwenzori is a word in a local dialect that means 'the rainmaker,' and the mountains affect the weather throughout the savannas of central Ta Ntchr. They are hidden behind dense clouds or mist for an average of three hundred days each year."

"Wow," I thought out loud, "that is serious."

Medjay Ipi continued, "Together with melted water from the glaciers, the abundant rainfall that flow from these clouds feed into the Hapy Eteru."

"Is it as tall as Kilimanjaro," I asked?

"Nn, no, Kilimanjaro is the Nswt Bety of the mountains of the moon. This mountain range is 120 km. [75 mi.] long and 48 km. [30 mi.] broad and around 5,109 m. [16,763 ft.] high."

"Look at those reeds of papyrus. They are over two meters [six feet six] tall."

"*Tiw,* some plants that are commonly found in temperate climates grow to enormous sizes here. These plants are able to grow to these heights on the uppers slopes of the mountains because there is no competition from trees. Lack of competition combined with abundant, year-round moisture, mineral-rich, acidic soil and high levels of Ra provide the conditions for this enormous level of growth."

Our royal Medjay cobra boat traveled swiftly around the curves of the river channel that leads from the Ruwenzori Mountains back into Hapy Eteru. Along the way, we saw a variety of animals, including the three-toed chameleon and sunbirds drinking nectar from lobelias and other flowers. We stopped once to pick tree-ripened wild bananas that melted in our mouths. I saw for the first time earthworms as long as ten meters (thirty-three feet) and as thick as a Medjay's thumb weave their way through the moist soil. As we reboarded our boat, we were followed by a gorgeous leopard that hid within the thick stands of bamboo, which provided cover for it. It followed us for maybe ten minutes or so before we lost it in the thick, deep tropical rain forest of Ta Ntchr.

Now I had seen all three mountains of the moon. Each provided its unique flavor and beauty to the Hapy Eteru. But what I had also learned was that not only did they provide Kemet with its vital water supply, but also they contributed to the people of Kemet and influenced our rich culture. This is also what my father and the chief Medjay wanted me to see and understand. *This experience was priceless,* I thought.

Once we reconnected back with the great Hapy Eteru, we traveled for two more days, only making two stops a day at several trading posts along the way to Khartoum. We watched the terrain change from tropical rain forest to vast grassland only to be swallowed up by a deathly desert. Once in Khartoum, we restocked our supplies and then on to Abu Hamed or Kurgus. Depending on the Hapy flood levels, we would leave our boats there and travel by foot across the eastern desert to the city of Kuban. Once in Kuban, we would travel by boat again to the temple of Kalabsha. There we would meet with the chief Medjay Jhutyms Ka-en-Heru and his elite Medjay forces. A forceful five thousand Medjay would be waiting at Abu just beyond the sixth cataract. From there, Chief Medjay Jhutyms Ka en-Heru would lead the entire fleet of Medjay forces from Abu to Waset. From Waset, the Medjay would rejoin with the Shemsu Heru Nswt Wahankh Inyotef, and the combined forces would engage our nothern enemies. This was the plan sent to Medjay Ka-en-Jhutyms by his father via his personal falcon messenger bird.

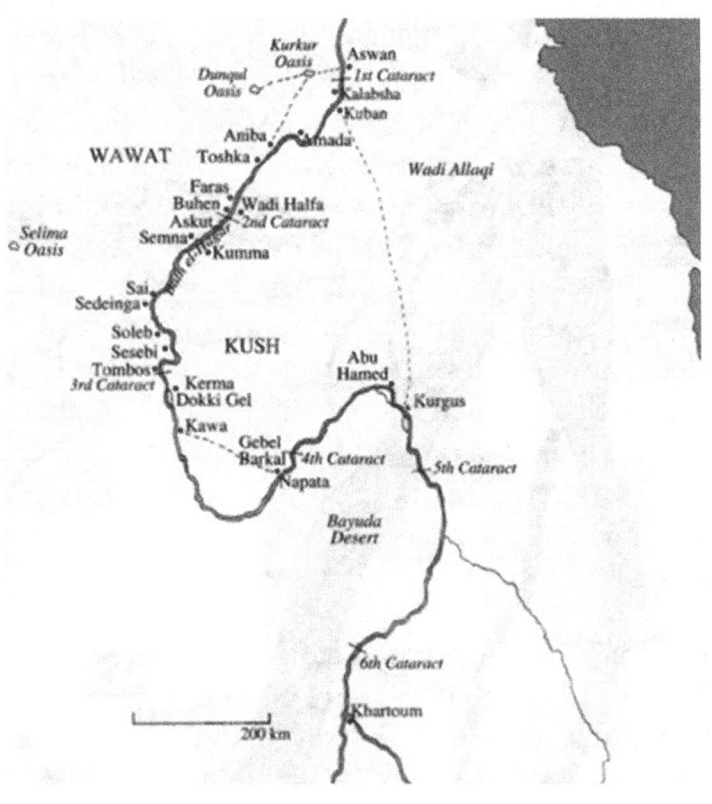

Medjay Sia-en-hotep explained the only possible spot to attack us would be when we travel by land from Kurgus to Kuban in the eastern desert. And the only warriors stupid enough to try that would be the Asiatics with their hired mercenaries, the Ta-Sety bowmen.

Medjay Sia-en-hotep raised his voice loud and clear, "Medjay, we shall destroy the Asiatics, and we shall teach our arrogant neighbors, the Ta-Sety bowmen, a lesson, never to fight against the Medjay again!"

The Medjay medju held up there spears in there right hands and with one resounding voice, yelled, "Dua Ntchr Mentchu!"

Just as planned, we arrived at Kurgus, met re-enforcements over twenty Medjay medju units, and picked up the neccessary supplies for our desert journey. Water stops and food were carefully placed along the trail every twenty-six miles along with several units of Medjay warriors all the way to Kuban. I felt like I had been trainning for this battle my whole life, and now it was almost near! Medjay Ka en Jhutyms instructed all the Medjay to gather in the Hapy Eteru for a final prayer before we leave its mighty shores to do battle.

We all stood in Hapy's ice cold water as Medjay Ka en Jhutyms spoke, "Mighty spirit, Divine Spirit of infinite power, spirit of infinite miles, spirit of infinite wisdom, the Creator that allows space to be concieved, knowledge to be comprehended, allow us your humble servants, the Medjay warriors, to be guided by you. By ourselves, we are nonexsistent. Through you, we are omnipowerful. Through you, nothing can happen to us. Through you, our journey will be powerful. Through you, our understanding will be liberating. Through you, Divine Spirit, we are already victorious. And because of our undying love for Ma'at, we are safe and we will return safe. Because Ma'at remains in our hearts the entire journey. Great and Divine Spirit, take hold of us. We have become one with you. As we hold each other's hands, we are one with the powerful, divine Ntchr, Amen-Ra."

Now we were ready for battle, and after that prayer, even I felt invincible. We walked in the formation of the shape of an arrow with our group at the tip. It was a very quick walk, almost a jog, but no one seemed to mind, not even I. And no one said a word. When we reached our first twenty-six-mile break, I asked Medjay Bennu Henenu why we did not take the river as it was much faster. He informed me that it was three times as dangerious. First the water was very high and unpredictable. Second we would have to pass three cataracts, giving our enemy three different chances to attack us, and we would be traveling through our enemies front yard. It was not smart at all. Now they must come to us in the desert, and in the desert, we are the masters. And they must attack us in between our stops or our Medjay scouts will inform us of their position, and if they are to have a fighting chance, which they don't, they need to surprise us.

"Will they attack us at night," I asked.

"No, the Asiatics would, but the Ta-Sety bowmen need the light of the day for there arrows, and they are the eyes of the foreign Asiactics," said Medjay Bennu Henenu.

On the second day, about two hundred kilometers just about halfway to Kuban, we saw three Medjay runners sprinting over the horizon in the desert sand like it was grass toward us. We knew that was a sign that the enemy was not far away. All the supplies were placed in one circle and burried in the sand so our enemies would not discover them. Our Medjay spies informed us that the Ta-Sety bowmen would attack from the left, forcing us to face them while the wild Asiatic swordsmen would attack from behind. Medjay Ka-en Jhutyms just smiled.

"You three, rest and prepare to do battle with us, bring forth our fastest runners," Medjay Ka-en-Jhutyms said to

Medjay Sia-en-hotep. Medjay Ka-en-Jhutyms gave them there instructions, and they were off. "Bring the falcons," Medjay Ka-en-Jhutyms said. Our best and fastest scribe, Medjay Khety, wrote out the plans as Medjay Ka-en Jhutyms told him. And the great falcon birds were off into flight with the messages. Medjay Sia-em-hotep called all the leaders together, and they gathered in a tight circular huddle. And Medjay Ka-em-Jhutyms drew his plans in the desert sand. It was very quick like everyone knew what to do already, then he gave a powerful prayer based on love of self, love of their nation, love of the divine and forgiveness.

"A strong warrior never uses hate to defeat his enemy, and the supierior warrior fights with love in his heart. We will celebrate the gift of life as we swing our swords."

Everyone yelled, "Dua Ntchr!"

"And if we feel pain, we shall grow stronger as we remember how acutely beautiful this life has been and how beautiful our next life will be."

"Dua Ntchr!"

"Remember the five dangers in battle, great Medjay: *Wa* [1], never lose your vision, *Senu* [2], never lose your story, *Shmut* [3], never lose your gifts or your special talents, *Fedu* [4], never lose your loving heart, *Diu* [5], never lose the Divine Spirit. Fight for these things, great Medjay, and tell the world that you'll never stop fighting for these things because that is why we were sent here."

"Dua Ntchr!" we all yelled.

"Fight with love, you mighty Medjay, and we shall win."
"Dua Ntchr!"

"Only those who fight with hate shall perish alone."

"Medjay!" He yelled, "Today,"—Heru and all the warriors together finished his words—"is a good day to die!"

Within ten minutes, we had broken into four groups, armed and ready. We advanced on our regular trail, ready for an attack. After about a mile into our journey, over the horizon came the Asiactics, screaming and waving their swords like madmen. Our troops fell into two horseshoe formations, facing both directions with shields up.

"Group one and three, shields up. Group two, blitz them with arrows at fifty meters!" yelled Medjay Ka-en-Jhutyms.

The sky was black from arrows raining on the Asian swordsmen, and nearly a quarter of their men fell or was injured before they even got to us. When they got to our shields, we clashed, then we let them in and clamped in on them, breaking them off into two groups. Every time Medjay Hu-sia raised his sword, an enemy fell, and his men drew inspiration from the fierceness of his assaults. Group 2 charged.

Group 3 was prepared for the Ta-Sety bowmen, and our shields were up like an umbrella. The bowmen's arrows just bounced off our large Medjay shields like raindrops. Quickly we charged with shields raised up. Meanwhile, our bowmen returned the arrow attack. Again the sky was black with arrows, and they had no shields to protect themselves. They tried to scatter, but we picked them off like flies.

Group 4, my group, charged the Ta-Sety bowmen with swords and spears, and within ten minutes, every Ta-Sety horsemen was killed or wounded. I must have killed three or four Ta-Sety bowmen myself.

Medjay Ni-Sobek and Medjay Bennu Henenu were at my side the whole battle, like they were almost glued to me along with Medjay Ka-en-Jhutyms. They formed a triangular pyramid around me, and I couldn't get hit if I wanted to. I saw Medjay Ka-en-Jhutyms cut two Ta-Sety bowsmen's head off with one swing of his sword as their blood splashed in my face. Finally, the Ta-Sety bowmen dropped there bows and surrendered, falling on their knees and begging for there lives.

"Tie them up," said Medjay Ka-en-Jhutyms. Group 4 reenforced the battle with the Asiatics, and at this point, fresh Medjay unit number 5 from the nearby camp came from behind the Asians, and now they were completely surrounded and destroyed in about twenty-five minutes of fierce fighting. At the end, no Asians were alive, not one. And we had captured maybe fifty or so Ta-Sety bowmen with maybe another twenty wounded.

I had read about the Medjay in battle and heard about the many legends of their triumphs, but this was even greater. We killed over 450 enemy warriors in about thirty minutes of fighting. The kill ratio was almost thirty to one, and we lost fifteen Medjay with eighteen wounded. But all the wounded would be ready for battle in the two-day journey left when we arrived at Kuban. Unbelievable! And we lost no one from our Medjay medju unit led by Medjay Ka-en-Jhutyms.

We took care of our wounded and dead, and we made the Ta-Sety bowmen bury their dead and the Asians' dead as well. Usually, the Asians burned their dead, but fuel was valuable, so they got a taste of the hot desert sand. We cared for the wounded Ta-Sety bowmen and tied there legs together and made them carry our supplies and all the extra weapons that we took from the dead Asian warriors as we marched them into Kuban with us.

Hundreds of Medjay warriors came out to greet us as we got about a mile from the great city of Kuban. We all marched in victory like we were celebrating the rise of Spdt (the Kemet New Year). Our group of Medjay medju was silent. They formed a pyramid around me, and at first, I didn't know what was going on. Medjay Sia-en-hotep told us that the real great battle had not started yet. I was taken to see the mayor of Kuban by my group, and they wanted to make sure I, the crown prince, was safe. I was a little annoyed because I wanted to be treated just like all the rest of these mighty Medjay warriors, but Medjay Ka-en-Jhutyms pulled me to the side and gave me a quick reality check.

"Listen to me," he said in a calm but stern voice. "Yes, you are Medjay, but even more important, you are the crown prince of Kemet, soon to be the Shemsu Heru Mentchu-hotep. And my job and our group of Medjay meju's mission is to return you to Waset, unharmed and ready to rule if necessary. Are you clear?"

I nodded my head in affirmation. I understood.

"Everybody is not who they seem to be. There are enemies in this town, and they want you dead. It would be a mighty victory for the north." He took a moment, then he continued, "What do you think that attack was all about in the desert? Their mission was to kill you, the crown prince. Five hundred men lost their lives just to kill you! So that Kemet would have no heir to the throne. So if the Nswt Intef was killed in battle,

Kemet would be in a state of chaos, confusion. Yes, so even among the mighty Medjay, the greatest warriors on earth and heaven, a spy or spies are within our midst. You will talk to no other Medjay outside our unit. When we reach the Temple of Khnum in Abu, my father will direct us from their. Until then the Medjay medju under my comand has but one voice, mine.

"Tonight we will sleep in the royal palace. It will be heavily guarded. Medjay Ka-en-Heru Bes and Medjay Khety-Ra, the two of you will prepare all our food until we get to Waset, no one is to touch our water or any of our gear. Is that understood?"

"*Tiw*, Medjay Ka-en-Jhutyms." They both spoke together as one voice.

Later that evening, after they had eaten, Medjay Ka-en-Jhutyms reviewed their plans very carefully with his Medjay medju, making sure each warrior understood there contribution to the overall success of this mission.

"Tonight we will sleep in a circle with our feet pointing outward, weapons in hand. Medjay Ni-Sobek, you will stand guard first outside our door. And, Medjay Bennu Henenu, you will post yourself near the window. Senior Medjay Sia-en-hotep and myself will replace you in three hours."

Medjay Ka-en-Jhutyms then reached into his bag and pulled out *medju* (ten) black cloths.

"Here, wrap these around your head and faces. If our attacker or attackers visits us tonight, they will not know which one of us is the crown prince." Smiles spread across the faces of the Medjay medju as they wrapped the black fabric around their heads and faces just below the eyes.

One of the Medjay said, "I'm the crown prince." "No," another said, "I'm the crown prince." "No, he's the crown prince."

They all chuckled for a moment.

"*Set* is the keyword for the spy. And, Medjay Ni-Sobek, if you hear us fighting inside, do not leave your post. There might be more than one Set." He nodded his head in affirmation.

"*Tiw*, Medjay ka-en-Jhutyms."

Later that night, when most of the Medjay were sleep except those on post, Medjay Ka-en-Jhutyms could hear a very faint sound like a brick sliding in the wall. He adjusted his sight in the direction of the sound, and he could see a dark opening about chest high in the wall. He touched the Medjay next to him, and the Medjay repeated the touch to the next Medjay until everyone was on their feet. It was soundless, and then a dark smoking object filled with a poison gas was propelled into the room. But before it could hit the floor, Medjay Ka-en-Jhutyms caught the object and threw it out the open window in one swirling motion. Quickly, Medjay Ka-en-Heru Bes shot a series of poison darts through the same small hole in the wall. Medjay Ka-en-Jhutyms pointed to three of the Medjay to quickly go to the adjacent room next to them from which the hole was connected. The Set (spy) was still there when they arrived, and the Set quickly threw several darts at the Medjay. But the Medjay deflected them all. Medjay Ipi rolled across the floor, moving toward the window to block the Set's escape, but with a fury, the Set attacked them with a long double-edged sword. The Medjay were amazed at the skill level of the Set as they were not able to strike him with their swords. They fought like the Ntchru with blazing speed in the night, but neither the Set nor the Medjay could penetrate the other's defense. The Set

151

pulled a whip out from his waist belt and, with blinding speed, wrapped it around Medjay Ipi's left ankle, pulling him off his feet. But Medjay Ipi quickly cut the whip loose with his skillful swordplay, and that was just enough time for the Set to leap through the window before the other Medjay could get to him.

Medjay Ipi said, "Don't follow him, it could be a trap."

As the three Medjay moved quickly to return to their room, Medjay Ni-Sobek stopped them.

"Do not enter, they are under attack. We must protect the outer perimeters."

Inside the room, Medjay Ka-en-Jhutyms blocked the window with his Medjay shield, and they had been showered with darts and arrows. But the skilled Medjay avoided them all.

"There is a Set unit," said Medjay Ka-en-Jhutyms. "Bring your shields. Medjay Sia-en-hotep, take the remaining five Medjay around back. Maybe we will end this fight tonight."

Medjay Ka-en-Jhutyms, Medjay Ka-en-Heru Bes, Medjay Mentchu- hotep, Medjay Ipi, and Medjay Akhtoy Ba-Heru all leaped out the window with their shields in hand, ready for an attack. They all landed almost silently and quickly fell into a Medjay V-formaton with shields up. But there was no attack. They scouted the area, but no one was to be found. And when Medjay Sia-en-hotep arrived with the rest of the Medjay unit, he reported the same. No one was to be found, not a trace, and the guards on post in the palace said no one passed them.

"Let's regroup inside, obviously this Set unit is extremely skilled, and they know this palace well"

"We just might be in the hyenas' den," said Medjay Ka-en-Jhutyms.

* * *

"Where is young Taa?" said Mistress Tany. The wife of the mayor of Kuban.

"I don't know, he was right behind me," said her eldest son, Sobek-en-sa-f.

"It must be the work of Medjay Ka-en-Jhutyms. He is the only one in their group skilled enough to capture young Taa, but he will not kill him. He will question him for information, I'm sure."

"They will not expect another attack tonight. We must kill the young crown prince before they reach the Temple of Kalabsha."

"Yes, before they connect with Medjay Jhutyms-ka-en-Heru," said Sobek-en-sa-f.

Behind the door, Medjay Jhutyms Ka-en-Heru had heard every thing, and it was time for action. With a quick explosive move taking the door off its hinges with the thrust of his palm, Medjay Jhutyms Ka-en-Heru was upon them. Mistress Tany threw her silver dagger, and Sobek en-sa-f, just as quick, launched three posion darts toward the Medjay. But Medjay Jhutyms Ka-en–Heru caught the dagger in his left hand and the darts, all three in his right hand and returned them to their masters. The dagger landed in Mistress Tany's left shoulder, and all three of the posion darts hit Sobek en-sa-f right in his heart as he fell to his knees. Mistress Tany swung her sword like she was not injured, but it was insignificant to Medjay Jhutyms Ka-en-Heru, who blocked the sword with his

153

bare right arm, pulled the dagger out of her shoulder with his left hand, and plunged it through her throat in two sweeping continuous motions. She dropped her sword as she reached for her throat, trying desperately to stop the gushing blood, but Medjay Jhutyms Ka-en-Heru grabbed her sword before it could hit the floor, and with only two mighty swings as he swirled into the air, both Mistress Tany and her son, Sobk-en-sa-f, were headless.

"Medjay Bennu Henenu and Medjay Ni-Sobek, go prepare a boat for us, not a royal Medjay boat. We want to be unnoticed in the dark of the night," said Medjay Ka-en-Jhutyms. "I think our attackers will strike again. They think we will not expect another attack so soon. They want to hit us on their turf. There might be other secret passages and unknown dangers waiting here for us. We will leave as soon as you can gather your gear," spoke Medjay Ka-en-Jhutyms.

Medjay Ni-Sobek grabbed his gear along with Medjay Bennu Henenu, and the two headed for the door. But as he reached to open the door, Chief Medjay Jhutyms Ka-en-Heru was standing there with a large sack in one hand. The whole Medjay medju was startled.

"Good plan, but we must change it," spoke Chief Medjay Jhutyms Ka-en-Heru. He threw the large sack on the floor and said, "Open it." Medjay Ka-en-Jhutyms nodded to Medjay Sia-en-hotep to open the sack. Medjay Sia-en-hotep opened the sack slowly and was shocked at first sight. The other Medjay looked on with suspense as he pulled the three heads from the sack one by one.

Medjay Ipi shouted out, "That one,"—as he pointed to the head of Taa—"was the Set we confronted in the next room. His sword skills were impeccable."

"I recognize the woman," said Ka-en-Jhutyms. "She is the mayor's wife, and these are her two sons."

Medjay Sia-en-hotep asked permission to speak, and the chief Medjay pointed to his son.

"You may speak," said Medjay Ka-en-Jhutyms.

"But why would the mayor do this? I know him personally, he is a friend of our family. And a friend of the Nswt Intef."

"We shall all find out the truth shortly. Pack everything up, and let's visit our mayor," spoke the chief Medjay Jhutyms Ka-en-Heru.

Medjay Ka-en-Jhutyms had to fall back on all his training at this point because he just wanted to run across the room and hug his father with all his might and just say, "I love you, Dad, and I miss you."

Instead he said, *"Dua Ntchr,* I'm glad you are here."

"And I am proud of you my, son, Medjay Ka-en-Jhutyms," as they all walked out the door and disappeared into the darkness.

* * *

The mayor felt a light touch shaking his leg gently. He thought maybe it was his lovely wife returning from her chores, wanting to have sex on this lovely full moon. He opened his eyes slowly. But as the mayor looked around, he was surrounded by the Medjay medju warriors.

Startled, he asked, "How did you get in here? Where are my royal guards?"

The chief Medjay Jhutyms Ka-en-Heru signaled for light. Medjay Bennu Henenu and Medjay Ni-Sobek lit several candles, and the room was bright.

"Honorable Mayor, we will ask the questions here tonight. Where is your lovely wife?" asked Medjay Jhutyms Ka-en-Heru.

The mayor stuttered at first, "She . . . she said she had some last- minute work that had to be done that could not wait for tomorrow and she would join me shortly."

"How well do you know your lovely wife, Mayor?" asked Medjay Jhutyms Ka-en-Heru. "And where is she from? Tany does not sound like a Kemetic or Kashite name."

The mayor tried to stand up, but he was pushed back down on the bed by Medjay Ka-en-Jhutyms.

156

"What is the meaning of these questions?" asked the mayor. "First, just answer them," with a stern voice, said Medjay Jhutyms

Ka-en-Heru.

"We, we have been married for only one year. She and her two sons are from Persia, but I think she told me she was Sumerian and that her forefathers were from Punt."

"That would explain their excellent swordplay," said Medjay Ipi. "How did you meet her?" asked Medjay Jhutyms Ka-en-Heru. "Our marriage was arranged by a neutral friend from the north,"

the mayor said.

"Where is that friend now, and what is his name?" asked Medjay Jhutyms Ka-en-Heru.

"He is a guest at the Kalabsha temple and is here to greet you and the crown prince tomorrow. He is a longtime admirer of your work and wants to talk trade. His name is Osorkon," said the mayor.

"He is Libyan then."

"Yes, I believe so, but what does this have to do with my wife? And where is she, do you know? asked the mayor.

"Yes, we do know her whereabouts. She is a spy along with her two sons, and they have been caught trying to assassinate the crown prince.

But we are trying to find out who put her up to this carefully planned plot. She kind of lost her head and can't talk right now, so anything you know would be helpful. And we will return her and her two sons to you tomorrow at the Temple of Kalabsha."

"This is ridiculous. My wife wouldn't hurt a fly," said the mayor.

The lights went out, and they were all gone as quickly as they came. The mayor looked into the palms of his left hand, and there was a black scarab—Kheper. The mayor ran to his door and opened it, and his two guards that were posted there said, "Can we help you, Mayor?" with their swords in their hands.

The mayor dropped his head in disgust as he looked at the scarab and said, "No!" as he slammed the door shut.

* * *

The Kalabsha Temple of Khnum

158

"We will travel tonight to the Kalabsha Temple, but only I will get off. Medjay Ka-en-Jhutyms and your Medjay Medju will continue on to Abu. Cross the sixth and last cataract in the morning light, but don't leave the water, and I will meet everyone in Abu at high noon. I'm sure plan B is to take place at the Kalabsha Temple. I will take care of this Libyan trader myself," said Medjay Jhutyms-ka-en-Heru.

When they arrived at the river, Medjay Ni-Sobek brought them an unmarked boat, and the eleven Medjay bordered quickly and guided there sails downstream toward the Kalabsha Temple. All was quiet, and once they were within eight hundred meters of the temple, Medjay Jhutyms Ka-en-Heru lowered himself into the Hapy Eteru and vanished underwater. Medjay Menchu-hotep looked amazed as there was no sign of the chief Medjay Jhutyms Ka-em-Heru.

"Is your father part fish?" he asked Medjay Ka-en-Jhutyms, and the other Medjay just smiled.

Medjay Jhutyms Ka-en-Heru saw two men dressed like Libyan warriors with a third man as they entered the Kalabsha Temple library meeting room where the mayor was already waiting with his two royal bodyguards.

"Where is my wife?" asked the mayor to the leader of the men.

"I don't know. I thought she would be here with you," said the Libyan.

"Medjay Jhutyms Ka-en-Heru said she was a spy caught trying to assassinate the crown prince. What do you know about all of these?"

"That's ridiculous," said the Libyan. "My men will find her for you. When will the Medjay and the crown price arrive?" asked the Libyan.

"In one hour," said the mayor, "in the royal front court."

The Libyan asked one of the mayor's bodyguards to bring the mayor some fresh water and sent one of his men to accompany him.

"I have a few gifts for you and your lovely wife from the north," said the Libyan. "Your man and my guard can bring them in before we meet the Medjay."

As the mayor's first bodyguard reached for the bucket of water in the well, the Libyan warrior snuck behind him and pulled out his knife. Just as he was about to stab the guard, Chief Medjay Jhutyms Ka-en-Heru grabbed the knife out of his hand and cut his throat with his other hand over the Libyans mouth, all without making a sound. He picked the Libyan up and placed him behind a wall and vanished without the mayor's guard noticing a thing. When the mayor's guard returned with the water, the Libyan was surprised.

"Where is my Libyan warrior?" said the Libyan to the mayor's guard. "I don't know. I did not see anyone behind me," said the guard as he served them water. Outside of the wall of the temple, the second Libyan warrior handed the mayor's second bodyguard a large heavy package. "You take that to the mayor, and I'll bring these other two," said the Libyan.

After the mayor's guard walked a few steps, the Libyan warrior pulled out his sword and aimed it at the guard's head. But just a few inches from contact, Medjay Jhutyms grabbed the sword as the headless Libyan warrior's body fell to the ground. The mayor's guard returned with the large package as he laid it down at the mayor's feet.

Now the Libyan called Osorkon was really getting angry. "Where is my Libyan warrior?" he asked with anger in his voice.

The guard said, "He is coming. He had two large packages to carry."

The Libyan walked to the doorway.

"Something is going on here," the mayor said.

"Yes, and it stinks. And it seems like you are hiding something." When the Libyan opened the door looking for his warriors, Chief

Medjay Jhutyms Ka-en-Heru was standing there. The Libyan was startled at first.

"Who are you? said the Libyan.

The mayor said, "That's Chief Medjay Jhutyms Ka-en-Heru."

* * *

Just as Ra rose over the horizon, giving light to Kemet, the Medjay medju reached the sixth cataract. There were hundreds of large rocks jetting out of Hapy Eteru, blocking their smooth passage.

"We shall carry the boat over the rocks," said Medjay Ka-en-Jhutyms. "This is almost impossible, but we are Medjay. We must focus and trust. The chief Medjay would say this. Focus on what? Focus on your intuition and your inner voice. Trust what? Trust that your great Medjay ancestors are leading you in the right direction. So let's get across these rocks and keep going, Medjay."

He knew either riverbank was dangerous, and traveling over the rocky mountains or through the Nubian village, there would be spies and a possible attack. With only the Medjay medju, his best line of defense was to remain in the rocky waters. He knew if there was an attack, they could see them one hundred meters away. The only real problem was to cross without damaging the boat or being eaten by Hapy crocodiles. With the water up to their necks as they sidestepped sharp, jagged rocks with a boat on their heads, the Medjay had to travel about eight hundred meters. Six hundred meters into their journey, Medjay Sia-en-hotep spotted a set of menacing crocodile eyes protruding out of the water, heading straight for them.

"*Sobek* at thirty meters north," Sia-en-hotep yelled out. "Stop here," said Medjay Ka-en-Jhutyms.

We all froze still in the waters as he placed his dagger in his locks on top of his head, then he placed a reed in his mouth and his spear in his hand and began swimming directly at the large crocodile.

Is this a suicide mission? I thought. Ten meters before contact, Medjay Ka-en-Jhutyms vanished underwater, leaving his water canteen floating in his place. The large crocodile opened his huge jaws to bite at the canteen, and as soon as his jaws opened, Medjay Ka-en-Jhutyms rammed his spear through his jaws and locked them together. He grabbed the crocodile's mouth and tied it shut with his belt, then he pulled out his dagger from his hair and gouged out the big crocodile's eyes as they spun around in circles at least three times. Now

Medjay Ka-en-Jhutyms swam underwater again and slit the crocodile's insides out until his guts floated in the water.

"Move toward the east quickly. The other crocodiles will smell the blood," Medjay Ka-en-Jhutyms yelled out to us. We moved as fast as we could on the jagged rocks with our hands numb, bodies ice-cold, and feet bruised with the boat still on our heads. Medjay Ka-en-Jhutyms dove underwater again, and when we saw him, he was pulling our boat ten meters in front of us. As the waters deepened, we climbed in the boat, exhausted but happy because we realized that once agan we had done the impossible.

* * *

The drums began to echo the sounds of life throughout the whole village, and the ceremony at the great Kalabsha Temple had started. Hundreds of people were gathered outside the temple walls just trying to get a glance at the crown prince Mentchu-hotep and the chief Medjay Jhutyms Ka-en-Heru. Five hundred Medjay warriors were split into two groups, one in front of the procession and the other half in the rear.

You could hear people in the crowd guessing, "Is that the crown prince?"

"No, it's that one."

"No, both of you are wrong, you fools. The crown prince is a giant, almost eight feet tall."

There was a sea of long white and red robes walking in double file into the courtyard. The leaders carried flagpoles and symbols from the various districts in southern Kemet and

Kash. They formed the outer wall of people inside of the great Kalabsha Temple courtyard. Next in line were a dozen or so long golden robes of the priests and priestesses of the Kalabsha Temple. Next came several dignitaries, ambassadors, and mayors of the neighboring cities. And toward the rear of this procession, dressed in all white were the all-female choir and musicians, chanting and singing hymns to the Ntchru. Last but not least were 250 Medjay warriors with another one hundred or so local warriors. What a feast for hungry eyes, all moving to the sound of the drum.

The large cedar doors remained open with the local and national flags flowing in the warm breeze on both sides of the great doors. Libations were poured by the elders, and they gave praises and thanks for our existence and for bringing us to this point.

"We honor you, great spirit, for the entire cosmos dwells within your spirit."

Water was poured, and the spirits were welcomed. The high priest gave the invocation as he gave the specific purpose of our gathering, the unification and healing of our two lands. Then the choir chanted hymns to Amen-Ra, and the dancers moved beyond the rhythm of the drums as they jumped and twirled in the air, electrifying the crowd. After the crowd calmed down, the lecture priest introduced the chief Medjay Jhutyms Ka-en-Heru after a long biography of his acomplishments. The crowd screamed as loud as they could, showing their appreciation, love, and affection for the great chief Medjay Jhutyms Ka-en-Heru. It took several minutes to calm them down again.

Medjay Jhutyms Ka-en-Heru pulled out the two swords from across his back holster and saluted the dignitaries and guests. And then he stood in silent prayer, facing the Ntchru

Khnum, Anuket, and Satet for about ten seconds. You could hear a pin drop—it was that quiet. He moved slowly and gracefully at first, with every eye on his intricate but deadly movements, and then he leaped what looked like ten feet in the air, twisting and twirling like no known creature on earth. His swords were moving so fast they were no longer visible to human eyes. Everyone's mouth just dropped open. In fact, the Medjay Jhutyms Ka-en-Heru at this point just looked like a blur of twisted wind and fire all blended into a luminous glow, and with a loud bolt of lightning shooting out into space from his sword, everyone covered their ears and dropped to the ground in fear.

When the smoke had cleared, the chief Medjay was standing on one leg with his right sword stuck in the ground through two feet of hard granite stone and his other sword in his left hand, pointing upward toward the sky with lightning reaching into the heavens emanating from it. What an awesome sight. No one moved at first. Babies and little children were crying, and people just looked in disbelief of what they had just seen.

Finally, the chief Medjay Jhutyms Ka-en-Heru placed his two swords back into their sheaths across his back, then he spoke, "It's better to have an Afrakan Kemet-Kash heart without words but with profound action than Afrakan Kemet-Kash words without a heart or dynamic action to back those words." He paused again for a few seconds. "The crown prince will not appear here today, but I can tell you, he is safe. I can feel his spirit just like I can see you. I will meet them in Abu, and we will join the Shemsu Heru Nswt Intef in Waset. And together we will crush our northern enemies, uniting our great and glorious country, Kemet-Sma Tawy, once again. So it has been spoken, so let it be written, so let it be done."

Every living soul was standing, cheering, laughing, and hugging each other. Young men and teenage boys and even little children, boys and girls, were saying, "I want to be a Medjay, a Medjay warrior." This time the flowing tears of the masses were of joy.

CHAPTER 8

THE RETURN HOME
TO WASET

As our boat entered the city of Abu, we could see hundreds of royal Medjay boats, and the city streets were filled with lots of friendly black and brown faces rushing about. All along the shore were Medjay and Kemet warriors going about their daily chores. You could kind of feel a friendly excitement in the air, and even though we were tired, everyone was alert and ready to hit the shore. We docked in the center of town, and I wondered, Would any of my family be at our home here in Abu. Medjay Sia-en-hotep spoke, "We will enter the southern temple of Khnum. They will be waiting for us, and there we will clean up, put on new clothes, and travel to the palace of Shemsu Heru Intef and Hemet Nswt wrt Iah. At the royal palace, we will eat and wait for the chief Medjay Jhutyms Ka-en-Heru to arrive. We will move as Medjay medju, and if approached by any other Medjay or Abu warriors or citizens or even priest, only Medjay Ka-en-Jhutyms will speak as our voice."

Once we bathed and put on new clothes, smiles came back to our faces. I had not seen some of the Medjay smiles since we left Khartoum more than one thousand miles ago.

When we reached the royal palace, I heard the guards yell out, "The crown prince has returned!"

My mother, the Hmt Nswt Wrt Iah, was the first to greet us. I had never really noticed how young and beautiful my mother was. Gold bracelets and rings adorned her wrists and fingers. She wore a small crown with a cobra protruding from above her pineal gland, highlighting her beautiful coco-brown skin and the royal Heru necklace around her long, slender neck. She greeted all the Medjay medju like a royal high priestess, and we all bowed our heads in respect and returned the royal hand salute. Then she stared at me for a moment, and tears came down her face. She knelt at my feet. I didn't know what to do, so I just stood there. She rose slowly and then gave me a big hug. I hugged her back, and we both kissed each other.

"Mother," I said. "My son," she said.

And we stayed in each other's embrace for a long while. She finally pulled herself togther, and she said, "Let me look at you. You have grown like a bamboo shoot."

All the Medjay medju laughed.

"You're taller than your father," she said. "Wait until your sister sees you."

"Where is my sister?" I said.

"She is in the Temple of Het Heru. She doesn't know you are here yet. She will be so surprised. All she talks about is her big brother, Medjay! The crown prince of Kemet day and night, she even dreams about you."

"Come on, Mother. I think you are overexaggerating," I said. "No, you'll see," she said.

"Medjay Ka-en-Jhutyms, may I surprise her?" "Go on," he said.

At first I did not recognize her. My cute little baby sister, my lotus flower, the royal daughter, had grown into a full woman. I was stunned. She was beautiful. No, she was breathtaking. I've never seen her with makeup and dressed like a royal priestess of Het Heru. She could not see me as I stood in the shadow of the palace doorway. Her face appeared soft and feminine, and her coco-brown body was lean and sculpted as her long white *lapa* wrapped around her perfect figure. I watched her graceful priestess walk as she sang hymns to Het Heru. She was as beautiful as my mother and Priestess Tem of Napata.

Once she got close to the door, I said "Ankh udja sneb neb" in my deepest voice. I saw the smile on her face.

"Brother, where are you?" she said. I stepped out. "Over here."

She ran as fast as she could and jumped into my arms.

"Oh, how I miss you, my brother. You are my world. I love you so much."

"And I love you, my princess."

Chief Medjay Jhutyms Ka-en-Heru led five hundred Medjay warriors into the great Temple of Khnum at Abu behind the sounds of drums. Once inside the courtyard, there were about five hundred more Medjay standing in formation, ready to greet their chief, and still four thousand more Medjay assembled outside the main gate. Without even seeing the enemy, somehow you knew that they, the Medjay, would not be denied victory.

A royal procession led by the priest and priestess and the royal family, guarded by Ka-en-Jhutyms's Medjay medju, greeted the chief Mejay. He knelt before the Hemet Nswt Wrt Iah as he touched the earth in front of her feet. She gripped a spear made of ebony wrapped with silver and gold and touched his forehead with the tip, then both shoulders, and then she asked him to rise as she then handed him the spear.

"You have already received the sacred sword of Kemet from my husband, the Shemsu Heru Nswt Intef. And now, I, the Hemet Nswt Wrt, Hem Sem Tepy of Het Heru and the Hemet of the Ntchru, bestow upon you the sacred spear of the Ntchr Mentchu, our Ntchr of war. May victory be ours. May our nation be united, and may all the people of Kemet enjoy Ma'at. And may we have continued peace and prosperity from Kash, our parent family from the south. Amen-Ra, Ptah-Khnum." And then five thousand Medjay wariorrs along with there chief Medjay all together chanted, "Amen-Ra, Ptah-Khnum, Dua Ntchru." That evening around the Medjay medju campfire, the crown prince Medjay Mentchu-hotep asked the chief Medjay Jhutyms Ka-en-Heru what happened to the mayor of Kuban and the Libyan Set.

The chief Medjay smiled.

"Everyone is where they are supposed to be. Ma'at has been restored," he said. "I crushed the Libyan Osorkan's death party for the mayor, who had no clue to what was going on. I presented the Libyan Osorkan with a gift, and when he opened it and saw his two guards' heads and the three Set spies' heads, the mayor's wife and her two sons, he was furious. He first threw several posion darts at me. I evaded them all with a smile. He grew even angrier, grabbing the sword from one of the mayor's bodyguards and thrusting it at me, then swinging desperately, trying to reorganize my body parts. I fought him empty-handed with only one hand, then after he was completely convinced that his skills were not as good as he thought they were and that he could not harm me, I broke his sword in half with my bare hands. He then pulled out a dagger and threw it at me. I caught the dagger and returned it with blinding speed to his upper chest.

"I didn't want the fun to end that soon. Then I took my royal spear and threw it through him, sticking into the back wall. He looked at the hole in his midsection in disbelief. He tried to reach for another sword, and I cut his hand off. Now that he was bleeding from the chest, stomach, and hand, I decided to end the show. As I stared into his eyes, I took his head. And when I presented his head to the royal court at the Kalabsha Temple, explaining the state of our enemies. It still had that stunned look on it's face."

Medjay Sia-en-hotep said, "All the Set heads had that same look on there faces, like they never knew their heads were gone." All the Medjay medju fell out laughing.

* * *

The royal princess Neferu was smiling in total joy just thinking about her brother's safe return. She floated next to a clump of floating lotus flowers inside her royal bath. The sacred flower of southern Kemet with light blue petals and yellow stamens sprouted upward from wide green leaves that rested on the water's surface. Princess Neferu used her royal baths not only to escape the blistering heat of Kemet, but also to relax because she had been so excited since her brother's safe return.

She could remember her brother telling her how the spreading leaves of the lotus flower symbolized the expansion of the soul. And that the lotus flower represented the five elements—its roots in the earth, its stalk in the water, its leaves in the air, its flower opening to the Ra fire, and its sacred scent the ether of the Ntchru. He'd also explained how the lotus flower was untouched by water as a pure being is untouched by *esfet*.

"I am his sacred lotus," she said softly, continuing to study the flower. She then touched the diamond Ankh necklace wrapped in gold that Mentchu-hotep had sent her from Ta Ntchr six years ago that hung from her neck. *His last words to me three and a half years ago, he said that I was his little lotus. That I always bloomed. I want to bloom for him now that I am a woman as his Hmt Nswt Wrt*, she thought.

* * *

As we boarded our vessel this time, it was not a dress rehearsal. We were at war. I was no longer in our fast small royal Medjay boat that I had grown accustomed to but a huge vessel that held several hundred men. It had sails over thirty feet high, beautifully decorated with images of Heru slaying Set. Along the sides of the vessel were stations for fifty rowmen on each side of the boat for when there was no wind or when traveling against the current. It was by far the most beautiful vessel I had ever seen. I took my place with the Medjay medju, and we were off in a flash. As I looked around, the Hapy Eteru was filled with dozens of these vessels and hundreds of smaller royal Medjay boats and several barges carrying more men and war paraphernalia.

We sailed into Waset like an invincible storm capable of desroying anything and everything in its path. Somehow, I personally felt invincible also now that I knew the look on my fellow Medjay's faces— proud, confident, and focused. This was what I did not understand before—my silly boyhood grin. That was what was going on—the smile was gone forever.

Our vessel and about twenty other ships stopped in Waset, and several commanders met with Medjay Jhutyms Ka-en-Heru. Afterward, the fleet split into two groups, one led by Medjay Ka-en-Jhutyms, who was to attack Iunet, and the other led by Medjay Hu-Sia, traveling to Abedju. Within ten minutes, they were off like a well-directed arrow.

When we hit the shore of Waset, there was much excitement in the air because everyone knew we were at war with the northerners. The streets were almost emtpy with the exception of a few merchants. First we went to the Nswt palace, but it was empty with the exception of a few servants. Our attention now was directed toward the sacred temple of Amen at Iput Isut. As we arrived at the front gate, which was heavily guarded with Medjay and Kemet warriors, the Hem Sem Tepy Dagi came forth to greet us. Words were exchanged between him and the chief Medjay, and then quickly, Medjay Jhutyms Ka-en-Heru took control, giving orders to his men and the guards. We walked quickly to the library where two other men were waiting.

For the first time in my life, I felt like a man, a Medjay warrior. I knew I would prevail in any test given to me. I was no longer afraid when I stood in the presence of great men. I knew that my time had arrived, and I could feel my great-grandfather's spirit next to me. When the chief Medjay called me into the library, I walked in with a great state of conscious competence. I felt a great spirit next to me, like my great-grandfather Shemsu Heru Mencthu-hotep was here with me.

"*Tiw,* my Neb," I responded with a quick stride. Four men stood in front of me now, three I knew well and the vizier, I only know who he is. They all looked at me, and I returned the look as I caught each men's eyes. First the Hem Sem Tepy Dagi, somehow he seemed shorter now. Then the vizier, I could tell he was not a warrior as his hands and body was soft with comfort. Then Medjay Akhtoy Ba-Heru from Punt, a great man as well as a super great warrior. And last but not least, the chief Medjay Jhutyms Ka-en-Heru, to whom there is no equal.

"We can feel you, Crown Prince Menchu-hotep." The Hem-Sem- tepy Daggi and his spiritual and physical guide Chief Medjay Jhutyms Ka-en-Heru and Medjay Akhtoy Ba-Heru could all feel a great energy surrounding the young crown prince. He was surely not the young boy who had left not long ago. He had grown not only physically, but mentally and spiritually as well.

When asked by the Hem Sem Tepy Dagi, "What more have you heard on your journey for knowledge?"

The prince stepped forward with his chest broad, oozing with confidence, and he responded reverently, "Hem-Sem-Tepy Dagi, when I listened most closely, I could hear the unheard, the sound of flowers opening, the sound of Ra's rays warming the earth, and the sound of grass embracing and drinking the morning dew. I began to hear not only my own heartbeat, but the beating hearts of my fellow comrades, like I can hear your heart now and the heartbeat of the scribe hiding behind the curtin taking notes."

Hem-Sem-Tepy Dagi spoke again, "How about the pain? Tell me about your training."

The crown prince knelt on one knee as he looked at the chief Medjay Jhutyms Ka-en-Heru.

"I know that you are the greatest teacher on the planet earth and that your life in itself is an impeccable book to be studied. You taught us that life was not meant to be easy, it's meant to be lived. Sometimes good, sometimes rough. But with every up and down, you learn lessons that make you strong. My training has taught me to look at the world like I am a spiritual warrior. And I have seen that the happiest people don't have the best of everything, but they make the best of everything. The common man has been taught that he has several senses, but as a Medjay warrior, we know there is only one sense—consciousness. We are all part of the one divine mind. What we call pain is just a reflective warning to bringing attention to the one sense, therefore, pain is an illusion that can be ignored on one hand and a gift on the other. And, Chief Medjay, your love of meditation has spread through my heart, and it has taught me that wise souls speak loudly in silence."

The Chief Medjay Jhutyms Ka-en-Heru and the Hem-Sem-Tepy Dagi along with Medjay Akhtoy Ba-Heru and the vizier nodded their heads approvingly.

"To hear the unheard," remarked the Hem-Sem-Tepy Dagi, "is a necessary discipline to be a good Nswt. For only when a ruler has learned to listen closely to the people's hearts, hearing their feelings and communicative pains unexpressed and complaints not spoken of, can a leader hope to inspire confidence in the people. This level of consciousness allows the leader to understand when something is wrong and meets the true needs of the citizens. The demise of countries come when leaders listen only to superficial words and do not penetrate deeply into the souls of the people to hear their opinions, feelings, and desires." "Medjay Akhtoy Ba-Heru, speaking on behalf of your Medjay medju, led by your brother, Medjay Ka-en-Jhutyms, tell us your verdict."

175

"It is with great pleasure and honor to be with this team. The crown prince is truly a Medjay in every sense of the word. He truly represents Ma'at, yet he is fierce like Heru and extremely intelligent, as well as a fast learner. Medjay Ka-en-Jhutyms gives his vote of approval of Medjay Mentchu-hotep. And, I, his younger brother, act as his voice. I would die for him, my Neb, and I know he would die for us. He is completely selfless. And yes, we all can see, Crown Prince, that your great-grandfather, Shemsu Heru Mentchu-hotep, stands with you."

Again I was shocked by their level of consciousness. Then Medjay Akhtoy Ba-Heru knelt at my feet and kissed them. Tears swelled in my eyes as I touched his shoulder, and when he stood, I hugged him. My whole life, I had been around people that loved me, but now I know what it means to love your fellowmen and your people.

The vizier spoke, "Warriors, our job is finish here. Crown Prince Mentchu-hotep, you shall lead your own vessel into war. Your father, the Nswt Intef, is waiting. I am confident that in his absence, you can lead our nation to victory and prosperity. So it has been spoken, so let it be written, so let it be done."

By the time our royal fleet arrived at Iwenet, we were greeted by several Medjay vessels. The Medjay commander pulled alongside our vessel and spoke, "Our work is done here. We have defeated our enemies. Your help is needed in Asyut and Abedju. We will clean up things here." Chief Medjay Jhutyms Ka-en-Heru asked, "Where is the Nswt,

Neb of Waset?"

"He has sailed to Asyut maybe one hour ago," said the Medjay commander.

Medjay Jhutyms Ka-en-Heru looked at his commanders. "How can I protect the Nswt if he charges out irresponsibly like a child with a new toy? His five dogs cannot protect him from the northerners. My fellow warriors, we make plans so that we have the best possible strategy to win, but we must follow those plans. Raise the sails. We must make up time. I will take half the fleet to Asyut. And, my son, you shall lead along with Medjay Mentchu-hotep the rest of the fleet to Abedju."

There was silence on the vessels as we cut through the waves of the Hapy Eteru with sailors and bowmen working together like I have never seen before. Soon Asyut was in sight, and we could see the smoke in the air and the sound of battle cries. The fighting was fierce, but our fleet followed closely behind Medjay Ka-n-Jhuty. It took another hour for us to reach our destination. As we approached our landing dock, I gathered all our men together on my ship. I didn't know what took over my body. I was running on autopilot.

I yelled out, "We are impeccable warriors!"

We all knelt on one knee, and I could see all the fleets were following us. At that moment, I became Shemsu Heru, and we all shouted out the warrior pledge.

We are impeccable warriors I see what cannot be seen

I feel what cannot be felt

I hear what cannot be heard

I know what is unknowable because I am the essence of all things

I will do the unthinkable because within me is the spirit of sovereignty

I live by the five laws of the spiritual warrior:
The law of responsibility, the law of love, the law of Ma'at,
the law of fearlessness, and the law of refining and giving
my gift.

I am a manifestation of harmonious intuition and strong
will.

I am Shemsu Heru in human form

A protector of the sovereign rights of my people A cultural
custodian

I am an ancestral spirit from ancient Kash and Kemet I am
the link to immortality

I am the past, the present, and the future I am the impeccable
warrior

I am Medjay!

And I shouted, "We will be victorious!"

We leaped and screamed so loud as we jumped out of those ships like we could fly. Our enemies almost started running when they saw our unbeatable spirits. Smiles came on our Kemet warriors, and they were charged by our presence. Arrows were flying by the thousands, and the number of arrows we unleashed against our northern enemies blackened the sky. They were clearly no match for the Medjay. Some of our Kemetic warriors had fought their way inside the gates and opened the huge cedar wood doors.

Medjay Ka-en-Jhutyms lead his warriors inside. My warriors finished the job outside. When we landed, they outnumbered us two to one, but thirty minutes into the fighting, the outside walls were ours. We had destroyed maybe five hundred northerners in that time. They simply were no match for our swords and spears in close-combat fighting, and our bowmen seemed to never miss, almost every arrow found a northern host. Even though half of the northern warriors were black and brown like us, they wore red-and-white cloth, which made it easy. Now their pale Asian partners were obvious enemies, and we had no mercy on them. Once we entered the gates, all we could see were bodies with red-and-white clothes. Medjay Ka-n-Jhuty had slaughtered his enemies and had sent some of his warriors to hunt down those who ran like scared dogs. At this point, they were putting out fires and stacking their enemies up in human piles. Medjay Ka-n-Jhuty looked at me and asked for permission to speak.

"Tiw," I said. What else could I say to one of the greatest warriors on earth or heaven?

"Amen-Ra is satisfied. We have returned another part of our sacred land back into the wings of Ma'at, and I wish we could continue north, my Lord, and finish this battle. But we must aid your father, the Nswt Intef. We arrived here in time to aid our Kemetic brothers bring victory and glory back to Kemet. My commanders in ships three and seven, you will stay here and bring order back where esfet once reigned. Stack their bodies back on the barges and vessels that brought them here and send it down north so our northern brothers can see what lies ahead for them. We will send more reinforcements when we find out the conditions of our warriors in Asyut. Shemsu Heru Mentchu-hotep, I kneel at your feet, for you fought today like the true mighty ruler of Kemet. Your father will be proud, and I am honored to be by your side."

All the warriors together yelled, "Dwa Ntchr, Dwa Ntchr, Dwa Ntchr, Shemsu Heru Mentchu-hotep!"

At Asyut, things were not going so good. The Kemet troops were divided and scattered. They underestimated their northern enemies with the help of the Ta-Sety bowmen, and the northerners had a slight advantage. The Shemsu Heru Intef was hurt pretty bad. He took a Ta-Sety bowman's arrow through his left shoulder, and he had a nasty cut on his left leg from a thrusting northern spear. It was a miracle he was still alive. When the chief Medjay Jhutyms Ka-en-Heru arrived, the first thing was to heal and care for the Nswt Intef while his elite Medjay troops went into full battle. He quickly patched up the Nswt's shoulder. The arrow went straight through, expanding, leaving a small hole in front and a big gash in the back. He could not tell if anything major was hit. He dressed it and placed his left arm in a sling. He cleaned the leg wound and dressed it. It was not bad, but it could have been a lot worse. It needed stitches. He wrapped it as tight as possible and made him a walking stick. The Nswt's dogs were by his side the whole time. The chief Medjay Jhutyms Ka-en- Heru placed the Nswt Intef on his back and carried him back to the ship and left part of his most trusted warriors to protect him with their lives. The tide had changed quickly once the Medjay arrived. The Ta-Sety bowmen tried to retreat, but Medjay Jhutyms cut off their escape route. First they attacked him with a blitz of arrows. Medjay Jhutyms Ka-en-Heru blocked all their arrows with his two swords while running toward them in a zigzag style. Once he was near them, all you can see were heads flying, twenty heads in all, a continuous whirl of circular blades. The rest of the bowmen threw down their bows and fell on their hands and knees in surrender style.

"Tie them up," the chief Medjay said. By now the morale of the northerners had been broken. The Medjay elite fighter cut through the northerners like hot butter. Within thirty minutes of hard fighting, the northerners were decimated. They threw down their weapons and begged for mercy.

"Tie them up," Medjay Jhutyms Ka-en-Heru said.

When Shemsu Heru Mentchu-hotep and Medjay Ka-en-Jhutyms arrived with reenforcements, the battle was over. Prisoners were tied up, and the dead placed in large human piles. Weapons had been collected and inventoried, and the wounded were being cared for.

"Where is my father?" said the royal prince Mentchu-hotep.

"Ship number one," replied Chief Medjay Jhutyms Ka-en-Heru. The royal prince Mentchu-hotep vanished in thin air in pursuit of his father. Practical or not, Medjay Ka-n-Jhuty just ran and hugged his father, Chief Medjay Jhutyms Ka-en-Heru. They hugged for a long time without any words said.

"Where is your brother?" asked the chief Medjay.

"Here, over here," Medjay Akhtoy Ba-Heru replied. Now the three of them hugged and touched foreheads with their eyes closed and smiles on their faces.

Once they arrived back in Waset, Chief Medjay Jhutyms Ka-en- Heru told Medjay Mentchu-hotep to check on the royal family and meet at Ipet Isut in two hours at the great temple of Amen. The crown prince said that he personally would take care of his father, the Nswt Intef. He then commanded his two sons to have all the troops ready for total war.

The two Medjay brothers greeted Medjay Mentchu-hotep with different eyes and with a different attitute.

Medjay Ka-en-Jhutyms spoke, "We saw your spirit today, and your spirit was a torch leading you out of darkness. Have no doubt that you can be the person you dreamed of being— that we also dreamed of you being. Feel it, believe it, become it, celebrate it. Know that your vision is *not* a mistake. The only mistake is not to follow it wherever it takes you."

"May I speak, my brother?" "Tiw."

Medjay Akhtoy Ba-Heru grabbed his hand in brothership as he spoke, "A rock is sure it's a rock. Gold is sure of its brilliance. Your belief in yourself must be just like that—rock solid. Trust what you feel, trust what you know, trust where spirit and your great Medjay ancestors are leading you. You are more than capable. Eliminate all doubt. Walk as our leader. Shemsu Heru. You are home now."

CHAPTER 9

SHEMSU HERU, MENTCHU-HOTEP NSWT NEB-KHRW-RA

Back in Waset, Nswt Hmt Wrt Iah and the royal princess Neferu led a victorious warrior prayer of over five thousand women at the sacred temple of Amen in Waset. Never had there been a gathering of women this large before in all of Kemet. Nswt Hmt Wrt Iah had taken on the role of all the great mothers. She was Sekhmet, the mate of Ptah; Het Heru, the mate of Ra; Mwt, the mate of Amen; Anuket, the mate of Khnum; and Ast, the royal mate of Asr. Priestess Neferu sings a hymn to Mentchu and her mother. The great mother Nswt Hmt Wrt Iah joins her on the second verse, and they are in perfect harmony as they kneel together.

"We stand and sing before you, Mentchu of Waset, and we know you hear our plea for you work only for Ma'at through Amen. We are not just silly women talking to a giant statue, but we are dynamic souls communicating with a dynamic spirit in which these statue are a representive of your greatness. We know that you are everywhere all the time because we can feel your energy everywhere we are all the time. So we call on you now, great Mentchu, comfort us and answer our prayers."

She waved her hands, and the multitudes of women all knelt in prayer position as they echoed each line of the prayer.

> *We give you praise to the height of heaven, And over the breath of the earth,*
>
> *I tell his might to traverse north and south, You are Amen, Neb of silence,*
>
> *Praise giving to Amen,*
>
> *We make for him adorations to his name, Who comes at the voice of the poor, When we call to you in our distress,*
>
> *You come to resue us,*
>
> *To give breath to those who are wretched, To rescue from bondage,*
>
> *You are Amen-Ra, Neb of Waset, Who rescues those who are in the duat,*

Who rescues those who are in battle for Ma'at, For you are he who is merciful,

When one appeals to you,

You are he who comes from afar,

Allow Mentchu to bring victory to Kemet, Who comes with the strength of Heru,

He whose face is strong among the Ntchru,

To make hotep over our two lands like Narmer, Heru appears as Nswt Bety,

Uniter of the two lands,

The two shores are made consant, Misconduct goes away,

Wrong is departed,

The land is in peace under its Neb,

He, Shemsu Heru Itef, gives disorder his back. Amen-Ra is satisfied,

Dwa Ntchr!

Everyone said, "Mrrrrrrrrrrrrrrrrrrrrrrr."

*   *   *

As our ships, boats, and barges arrived back in Waset, it was a quiet homecoming even though we were victorious in battle and had beaten our enemies of the north. Kemet was still divided, and the Nswt was badly wounded. Thousands of women and children waved and threw flowers at us as we sailed into the main harbor at Waset, leading to the great temple of Amen-Ra. We walked with purpose but in silence.

Chief Medjay Jhutyms Ka-en-Heru immediately called a meeting of the elders, the priests, the members of the royal Court, the royal family, and all his commanders and officers. Outside the temple of Amen, Iput Asut, in Waset, you could hear a pin drop. Security was at its maximum. The royal family sat in chairs, and everyone else sat in a semicircle around them on mats in the open courtyard.

Chief Medjay, the eldest by far, spoke first.

"We must accomplish five things before we leave this circle, my people, my family. *Wa* [1], we must swear in Mentchu-hotep as coregent and Shemsu Heru of Kemet to rule alongside his father, Shemsu Intef, who is badly wounded at this moment. *Senu* [2], we must arrange for the wedding of the crown prince to the royal princess to secure his position as the Nswt of Waset and all of Kemet. *Shmut* [3], Hmt Nswt wrt Iah, I recommend that she become the Mwt Nswt Ntchrt wrt, the great royal mother of the Ntchru of Kemet, the wife of the Ntchru with much expanded duties. *Fedu* [4], a viceroy, the royal ambassador of Kash, is to become part of the royal court and a member of the advisory team along with the great elders and priest. We must expand our borders north and south. We must heal and grow at the same time. *Diu* [5], we must send heavy reinforcements quickly to Abedju to secure our new borders, to prepare for continued war, to reunite all of Kemet, and to prepare to build a city powerful enough to launch our next attack to unite all of Kemet."

You could see without anyone saying a word that the royal court was in total agreement with the chief Medjay. He continued after a short pause.

"Before we hear from Shemsu Heru Intef and the crown prince Medjay Mentchu-hotep, I want to say only a few more words on patience. Our young crown prince was born with the wisdom of his great-grandfather Mentchu-hotep, who founded this city and established the royal family here. But these were only seeds that became a golden egg of hope. We have been patient with his development over the last nineteen seasons of the inundation of Hapy since his birth and the great rulership of his father, Shemsu Heru Intef. He has proven himself worthy of his great name. He has excelled in his first level of his rights of passage by one of our greatest teachers, the high priestess Hmt Nswt Wrt Iah of the temple of Het Heru. He has excelled in education through the sacred temple of Amen, priestship, under the divine guidance of the high priest Hem Sem Tepy Dagi. He has excelled as a Medjay warrior under the leadership of High Commander Medjay Ka-en-Jhutyms of Barwat. And he has proven himself a great warrior already in two major battles with our enemies."

The whole royal court stood and chanted, "Dwa Ntchr!" They cheered with great enthusiasm for they knew his time had arrived. Hmt Nswt wrt Iah squeezed his right hand and smiled at him with so much motherly pride she could burst. But the royal princess Neferu threw her arms around her brother with uncontrollable tears of joy.

"Family, it is now time for action!" shouted the chief Medjay Jhutyms Ka-en-Heru.

Again a resounded "Dwa Ntchr" came from the royal court. "Patience is unlimited will. Will is an unconquerable force that rest at the feet of all success. If one waits long enough, if your will is strong enough, even an egg will walk." The courtyard chuckled as the chief Medjay paused.

"Endurance is the soul of patience. One moment of patience may ward off great disaster. One moment of impatience may ruin a whole nation. The seeds of Shemsu Heru Menchu-hotep has grown into a golden egg, and this golden egg has walked." With his fist thrusted into the air, Everyone stood again.

"It is time for action, Shemsu Heru Mentchu-hotep!" he shouted.

The vote of approval was swift and quick with much excitement and enthusiasm. The task of point senu was given to the royal family and the priestship of the temple of Amen-Ra and Het Heru to come up with a time and date of the royal wedding as quick as possible. The meeting lasted about five hours with most of the time devoted to points *shmut* [3], *fedu* [4], and *diu* [5]. New positions were quickly filled, and most of the appointmens were made by Shemsu Heru Mentchu-hotep with the guidence of Hem Sem Tepy Dagi and the chief Medjay Jhutyms Ka-en- Heru. When the meeting ended, smiles had returned to the faces of the leadership, and the joy quickly spread to the masses of the people of Kemet.

* * *

"I have nothing to wear, I mean really, I am so not ready. What am I going to wear, Mother?" Neferu said with her hands in her hair.

"Calm down, Neferu, we will send for Priestess Tem. She will make you something gorgeous."

"Thank you, Mother. You are so wise. I'm going to need you more than ever," Neferu wrapped her arms around her mother.

"Actually, it's you, Neferu, I'm going to need more than ever," said the great royal mother of the Ntchru. "You are the smartest girl in all your classes, the new high priestess of Het Heru and the Hmt Nswt Wrt of all of Kemet, the strongest nation on earth."

"Mother, this is too much too fast. I'm going to faint."

* * *

"Medjay Ka-en-Jhutyms, may I have a word with you? What's in the Medjay manual about marriage?"

"I don't want to disappoint you, Crown Prince Mentchu-hotep, but I'm not the one to talk to about such things. I have no experience in these matters. I would yield to senior Medjay Sia-en-hotep or my father. Matters concerning women and marriage, this is way out of my league. I have mastered many things in my short physical encounter here on this planet, but women, I have avoided like a plague. They seem to cloud my force field, and they don't respond correctly to logic. So for the moment, young prince, my advice would be to talk with your own father who has already walked in the path you are traveling."

"Dua, Medjay Ka-en-Jhutyms, for that was great advice." I bowed my head to him.

"May Amen-Ra continue to guide you, *ankh, udja sneb neb.*"

* * *

"You look fantastic, Hmt Nswt Wrt Neferu," said High Priestess Tem from Napata.

"Thank you so much. I would have been a mess without you." "You are truly my best friend in the world," said High Priestess

Neferu as they hugged each other in great joy, laughing and spinning around in circles.

"Now let's have some order here, young priestess, before you kill yourselves in happiness and there won't be a wedding." Then she started laughing. Mwt Nswt Ntchrt Wrt Iah, the great royal mother of the Ntchrw, joined in on their fun. Now all three of them were hugging and spinning around in circles.

"Medjay Bennu Henenu and Medjay Ni-Sobek, will you stand next to me at the royal wedding?" They both looked surprised.

Medjay Bennu Henenu spoke first, "It will be a royal honor to stand next to you, Crown Prince Mentchu-hotep," as he bowed his head in respect.

"I am humbled and speechless, Crown Prince, *tiw*," said Medjay Ni-Sobek as he knelt on one knee.

"This will be my first wedding ever," said Medjay Ni-Sobek. "Me too," said Medjay Bennu Henenu.

"I don't get it," said the crown prince. "You have traveled and fought on three continents, climbed to the top of the mountains of the moon, spoken to kings, and even slayed dragons, fought in a dozen battles, but you have never been to a wedding?"

* * *

"I came to give you just a little motherly advice, Priestess Neferu." They both sat down and smiled at each other. "To keep a marriage healthy, the first thing is to honor the relationship itself. Come to it as something led by Divine Spirit. The next step is to acknowledge each other's sacred souls. You don't have a soul, Neferu. You are a soul, and you have a body. Acknowledge each other not just as human beings but also as divine souls who have chosen a body to come into. Acknowledge your divine mate as the ruler of all Kemet and the world and you as the great royal wife. Then through ritual, bring these two divine souls together as one for eternity." Mwt Nefer Wrt Eah smiled at her daughter. "This too is divine work." She smiled with joy bubbling in her heart as they embraced.

* * *

"What do you think of my bow skills, Medjay Ahktoy Ba-Heru? Nineteen out of twenty bull's-eyes. I respect your opinion since no one outside of your brother and father's skills surpassed yours that I've met." "I don't think so because you have seen my mother in action when we were in Punt."

"*Tiw*, I forgot about her."

"Wow! Where should I put all these royal gifts, Shemsu Heru Nswt Mentchu-hotep?"

"First of all, Medjay Ahktoy Ba-Heru, a new member and commander of chief Medjay Jhutyms Ka-en-Heru's elite Medjay forces, you are not my personal servant. You are head of security for the royal palace and royal family. Secondly, it is I who should be kneeling to you, big brother, after all your help and guidance. And thirdly, I have no idea where we are going to put all these gifts."

"Have you looked outside? They are still lined up for a hundred meters at the door of the royal palace with royal gifts, and the royal wedding was last week, ten days ago. I think you should commission a team of workers to add a new wing onto the royal palace," suggested Medjay Ahktoy Ba-Heru.

"Great idea, I shall talk to Hmt Nswt Wrt Neferu. She loves these kinds of innovations and improvements. Maybe we will add two new wings to the royal palace."

Members of the royal court from Kash, bringing gifts for Shemsu Heru Nswt Mentchu-hotep and Hmt Nswt Wrt Neferu

* * *

Shemsu Heru Mentchu-hotep and Hmt Nswt Wrt Neferu walked through the sacred temple of Het Heru as husband and wife. As they passed a circular pond full of lotus flowers, he took her hand. Warmth spread between them, causing them to smile as one soul into the darkness.

"You are the Hemt Sem Tepy of this sacred and divine temple, Neferu, and I am so proud of you." For a moment, she was speechless, and tears rolled down her eyes.

"I am so happy. I have dreamed of this moment, of us walking together as one my whole life. The Ntchru has granted and answered all my sacred prayers, and I want this to be the beginning of a never-ending story." He held Neferu close to his heart.

"We must go within and listen in the silence. Listen with awareness in the stillness. We must relax our bodies, quiet our minds, and enter the sanctum within as one," Shemsu Mentchu-hotep replied as he stared into Neferu's eyes. They watched Ra slide below the horizon embraced in each others arms as the world went dark as one.

* * *

For the next month, Neferu and Mentchu-hotep spent almost every available moment together that they could find. They took long walks together every other day after dinner, and Neferu even had a special boat made for them so they could cruise the Hapy Eteru or down a special canal, which was dug just for their pleasure.

"The royal palace has never looked better, Hmt Nswt Wrt Neferu, you are a genius."

"Well, I can't take all the credit. Mother and Hemt Sem Tepy Tem of Napata helped a little." They both smiled.

"You know the royal architect from Napata, Hem Tepy Kha-f-Ptah? He is quite an amazing man. He seems to know what I want even before I finish explaining it. I think he can read minds. Strange but amazing," she pondered.

"With the three new wings, I can invite all the Medjay in Napata over for the weekend." Shemsu Heru Mentchu-hotep fell out laughing. Neferu did not think it was that funny. "I was only playing, Neferu. It looks wonderful."

"Do you remember the divination reading Mother did before you left for Medjay initiation?"

"*Tiw*, you know I do. Everything she said came true. Why do you ask?" "I just did a reading in the sacred temple of Het Heru, and it talked about your uniting Upper and Lower Kemet on your fourteenth year on the throne."

"Well, sometimes it can be wrong, because I'm going to unite our two lands within the next two years."

Hemet Nswt Wrt Neferu looked into her husband's eyes. "Divination teaches us to look beneath the surface to see what's really happening. At times, your own eyes might deceive you. Your ears might deceive you. Others may deceive you. But through divination, your ancestors and the Ntchru will reveal the truth. The truth is sometimes bitter, but we must learn to embrace it."

* * *

"Son, this may be our last conversation on this physical plane. I can feel life slowly slipping away. I can feel the ancestors calling me. And I need you to stand strong, son."

"No, Father, it is not time yet."

"Kemet needs you to stand strong, son. Your family needs you to stand strong." He coughed and slowly tried to capture his breath. He continued, "As outside negative thoughts appear, reject them and tell them to go away. Do not allow them entrance into your temple. Live in the thought world of your higher self, and open your mind to the influx of cosmic ideas. Add resource to your warehouse—reading, study, contemplation and concentration, and silence. The world of ideas is the world of the higher mind. We honor the ancestors, but it's not just about honoring them, it's also about honoring *you* and *your* potential. The ancestors are a source of light and can see your potential better than you can. This is why it's crucial to maintain that communication with them. What are your ancestors trying to tell you? Are you listening, son?"

Shemsu Heru Mentchu-hotep handed his father a golden cup filled with water and held his head as he watched him drink it slowly. He thought how much he loved this man who has given him so much and has sacrificed for him so much. And when no one else could give him advice on how to be a good husband and a great ruler, he was there for him.

His father continued, "A day does not go by without a visit from the sacred ones, your ancestors, and yes, I can see my grandfather standing next to you, my son. The Ntchru are all around you. Pay close attention. The signs are all around us and can appear in any form, any shape—a bird circling above the royal palace, a sudden spark of inspiration, advice from your sister, your beautiful wife, a kind word from a stranger, a miraculous answer to a problem, the reading from a divination. Don't listen with your ears, listen with your heart and mind, my son. Your loved ones in spirit have full confidence in you, and you can count on their support. But you must also have full faith and confidence in yourself as the Shemsu Heru Nswt Bety Mentchu-hotep, Sa Ra Neb Kheperu-Ra." He felt his father's life force slip away as his hand went limp inside his.

"No, Father, you can't leave me yet. I have so much to say, so much to tell you." He held his father in his arms, just rocking for a long time before his mother pulled them apart.

That evening after the high priest Hem Tepy Dagi came for his father's body, it was Nswt Hemet Wrt Iah who could not stop crying and Mentchu-hotep who held her.

"Mother, it's all right, I will take care of you and Neferu. I promised father I would stand strong."

"I *Mrrr* you, Neferu."

"And I have always loved you, Mentchu-hotep, even before I knew what love was, I loved you. And even before I loved myself, I loved you." "Look at you, you have grown into a gorgeous Hemt Nswt wrt, Neferu." "Mother taught us that beauty catches your attention, but character catches the heart. Mentchu-hotep, you have my heart." She stared at her husband. "I can feel your strength across the room, Shemsu Heru Mentchu- hotep. There has not been a ruler like you on the throne since Shemsu Heru Peppy, and that's been over 150 years ago." She sat down next to her husband and held his hand. "And like me, even the common people can feel your strength, your leadership, your sense of caring. And that's why they, the people of Kemet and Kash, will follow you anywhere and even die for you."

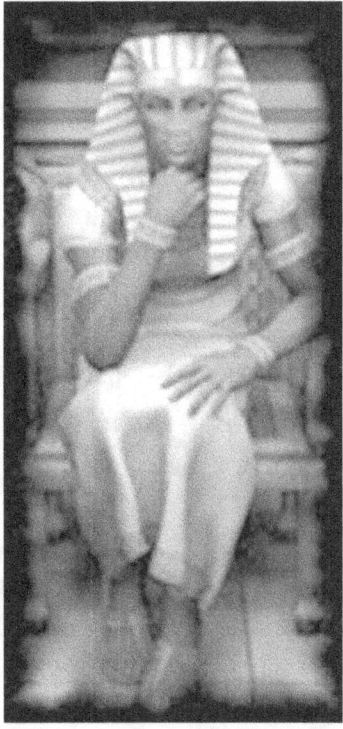

Shemsu Heru Mentchu-hotep

"Whatever I've learned, I've learned from them, the people of Kemet and Kash. And my strength, I owe to the Medjay and Father. And most of all, Neferu, it is you and Mother that has taught me to love unconditionally." Her hand tightened around his.

"You see? It is your selflessness and total devotion that will make you one of our greatest Nswt Bety ever."

"And with you by my side, Hmt Nswt Wrt Neferu, I will unite our nation and bring prosperity to unknown heights." She smiled at her husband's pride and confidence in her. "Neferu, your mangement skills and organizational skills have even past mothers, and even the chief Medjay Jhutyms Ka-en-Heru says she's the best." She looked away.

"And yet I am not enough."

"What do you mean? You're my life, Neferu."

"You have been the Nswt, Shemsu Heru for five years since Dad died, and you have made our country stronger than it has ever been since our great-grandfather established the royal family here at Waset. You have rebuilt Waset. Even the priest are saying Waset is the eye of Ra with its beautiful temples unmatched anywhere in the world. You have expanded trade all the way to the mountains of the moon. But you need an heir to the thrown, and I cannot give you one. Perhaps it is time to take another wife."

Mentchu-hotep stood up, placing both his hands on her shoulders, then placing his right fingertips under her chin and gently lifting it.

"Without you, Neferu, there is no vision. Without vision, Kemet will perish." She kissed his hand gently.

"I don't want our nation to perish," she said.

"Then stay beside me, Neferu. I need you as my Hmt Nswt Wrt. Always stay beside me." A beautiful smile gleamed from her magnificent face.

"I'm a part of you, Mentchu-hotep. I was born to be part of you. the Ntchru sent me here as your gift. Not beside you, but within you. Like a great spirit, like our great-grandfather as he remains within you, as he always have and always will. I am within you." They pulled each other so very tight together and hugged for a long time.

He looked deep down into her almost totally black eyes and said, "*Mrrr e etch*. I love you, and I feel you."

"And I feel you, my Nswt.

* * *

"Hem Tepy Kha-f-Ptah, please come and sit down."

"Is everything all right, my Neb?" he asked with a concerned look on his face.

"Dua Ntchr, everything is *eqker*, excellent." I stared at him for a moment, and I noticed the same twinkle in his eyes as the chief Medjay Jhutyms Ka-en-Heru.

"I am puzzled. You are working with the hardest granite and diorite stones known to man, and yet when you are finished, it's like you were working with soft soapstone. Are you training our priest to do this work? A visiting priest from the north and master mason from the sacred temple of Het Ka Ptah commented that the knowledge that you posess he thought was lost with the ancient ones. It is unknown to him and to any one he knows on how the letters and figures were elaborately embossed and counter sunk in granite. He was astonished. He admitted to me that no one could do this by hand, and yet you have done it." I paused for a mintue to recapture my thoughts. "Before you answer any of those questions, are you related to the chief Medjay Jhutyms Ka-en-Heru?"

He looked up at me, surprised at first, then in his usual calm voice, he said, "His second daughter is my mother, Neferu-Rat."

"*Tiw,* now I know why you can do these things. You are an initiate of the immortal Psju and a direct descendant of the original Annu people through your bloodline, and you have read the Emerald Tablets and the forty-two books of Jhuty and countless other books beyond my knowledge."

"To the untrained mind, what they cannot perceive always seems impossible until it's done," said Hem Tepy Kha-f-Ptah. He stood up. "I trust what was said here was never said. If my work pleases you, my Neb, I will continue."

"Your work pleases me very much, Hem Tepy Kha-f-Ptah." We bowed to each other.

* * *

"May I touch your stomach, royal wife Priestess Tem? I am so happy for you."

"No, it is I that is so happy for us." They hugged each other with so much love. "I'm having this baby for you, Hemt Nswt Wrt Neferu."

"What do you mean?" she asked.

"I know you can't have a baby with your brother, and I know how much you love him. That's why I'm so afraid, Neferu."

"What are you afraid of, Priestess Tem? You know we have the best healers in all the land at your side."

"What if the child is a girl?"

"If you have a daughter, you shall do three things."

"What?" asked Priestess Tem.

"Pray to the Ntcht Taurt that she is healthy and wise like yourself. *Mrrr* her, I mean really love her with all your might. Love her more than you do yourself. And become pregnant once again because while a daughter will give us countless joys and continue our bloodline, our nation Kemet needs a son right now. Any healthy child is a miracle, containing the memories, hopes, and delights of both the present and past consciousness. But without a son, there is no heir to the throne of Kemet, and where there is no heir, our future vision is blurry. A nation with a blurry vision is a doomed nation."

"That's why I love you so much. You have always been so much smarter and wiser than your years." She hugged Neferu again. "You're my big little sister." They laughed like they always do in each other's company, and they hugged like their lives depended on it.

"Hmt Nswt Wrt Neferu, you know we are closer than blood sisters. You are my best friend in two worlds, in infinite worlds, and I would truly die for you!"

"And you know I love you too, Priestess Tem."

"But can I share my deepest secret with you?" Neferu stopped and sat down next to her best friend and cowife, holding her hand.

"Of course."

"I know that Shemsu Heru Mentchu-hotep likes me, no, I know that he does loves me. And he is always so kind to me. He has always been kind and loving."

"I think that is his nature," said Neferu.

"What I'm trying to say is that when he is with me, I think he is with you." Neferu squeezed her hand as she looked into her best friend's eyes.

"What do you mean?"

"The two of you share a love that is so beautiful and so wonderful that even when I think of it, it brings joy to my heart. But at the same time, I am so jealous. And I am so ashamed of myself for that. That is not Ma'at. I want to live in Ma'at, Neferu, because I love both of you so much."

"He loves you too, royal Priestess Tem, and he respects your talents and gifts. He speaks about your great healing powers and your soothing touch even to me, and I am so happy for your bond. When I told him he needed another wife, he mentioned you, Priestess Tem."

"He really did?" "Tiw."

"You are such a special person, Hemt Nswt Wrt Neferu. I know that you love Mentchu-hotep more than life itself and you always have. Even when you were five years old, the only thing you wanted to talk about was the crown prince Mentchu-hotep. You loved him so much you made me love him before I ever saw him. And when I did finally meet him, I could see exactly what you saw in him. *Tiw,* he is so special like you. You two were made in heaven for each other, and I am so honored to be loved by both of you. It will take several lifetimes to repay my debt to you both."

Priestess Neferu placed her hands on Priestess Tem's belly, and she began to sing.

"Excuse me, my royal Nebut, I will come back at another time. I have finished the new courtyard and sacred pool in the royal palace," said Hem Tepy Kha-f-Ptah.

"Royal ladies, do not worry. It's a beautiful boy, and he said his name is Mentch-hotep. But what was just said was never said, so you will share it with no one. *Ankh Udja Seneb Nebut.*"

After a long workout with the Medjay medju, we all bathed in the Hapy Eteru together. Afterward when I returned to the royal palace, I rinsed off in our private sacred pool that Nswt Hemt Wrt Neferu had specially made just for us. Everything she touched gleamed with beauty. The Ntchru knew that beauty would produce beauty. Our whole royal palace was stunning. He walked softly unheard into the royal sleeping chambers like a Medjay, smiling at his royal wife, Neferu, as she slept. She was sleeping in the Asrian position with her arms folded and her feet together. How blessed he was, he thought as he looked back over his life. Not one beautiful wife, but two beautiful women and a young strong son.

Thank you, Great-Grandfather. He bent over to kiss Neferu on her forehead.

"Father, why are you so tall?"

"Because my great-grandfather, Shemsu Heru Mentchu-hotep, was tall, and I was born in his image, his likeness."

"Will I be tall like you since my name is Mentchu-hotep also, Father?"

"*Tiw,* you will no doubt be tall like me, son." "Where is he now, Father, your great-grandfather?

"He is a great and special spirit called an ancestor that is always with us and protecting us, but we just can't see him."

"Why?"

"Because ancestor spirits are invisible, Mentchu-hotep." "Why is he an ancestor?"

"Because the great Creator gave him a powerful mission, and he died before he finished his mission."

"Why?"

"Because he started something great that was not completed, so when my father could not complete that same mission, it became my job to complete it. And he is watching us all, even right now."

"Are you sure, Father? I can't see him."

"It's like the wind, you can feel it, but you cannot touch it or see it." "So your great-grandfather is a wind spirit?"

"I guess you could say that."

"Can I help you and your great granfather complete your great mission, Father?"

"I'm counting on it, son. I'm counting on it . . ."

"The food was especially good tonight, Neferu, even little Mentchu- hotep ate all his food and asked for seconds, Dua Ntchr."

"Well, you can thank your royal wife Priestess Tem. She cooked everything."

"No, not everything. How about my special date-and-honey dish that only you can make?"

"I showed her how to do it, and she did it." "She is really special."

"I told you she was."

"All right, we both agree she's special." Nswt Hemt Wrt Neferu smiled.

"Neferu, do you think I can borrow our chief architect Hem Tepy Kha-f-Ptah tomorrow? You and the royal Hmt Tem have been really keeping him busy lately. I want to discuss some sacred burial plans on the west bank for the four Shemsu Heru of Waset."

"Nefer, because I want to discuss your sacred resting place with him also."

"Do you miss the great royal city of Napata, Nswt Hmt Tem?" I asked as we walked in the courtyard of the royal palace.

"*Tiw,* yes and no. I miss my brother, Prince Piye. He was so kind and patient with me. And my little sister, Princess Kawit, who is growing into a beautiful young lady. But just like your mother took care of me, Princess Kawit will be working with our mother to complete her priestess training starting next month. Most of my family is here, my eldest brother, Medjay Ipi, my father's two brothers, several of my priestesses from the temple of Het Heru, my favorite architect, Kha- f-Ptah, and you are here, my Neb. And whereever you are, my Neb, I will be satisfied, blessed, and honored." She held his hand and kissed it. "I am pleased that you are happy, my Hemt." Shemsu Heru Mentchu-hotep picked a yellow Orchid flower from their flowing water fountain in the center of the courtyard and placed it in her hair. "Thank you for being a part of our life here in Waset, and yes, I do love you.

And I think you are very special."

"I know I have said this to you before, my great Neb Shemsu Heru Mentchu-hotep, that I *Mrrr* you and your great impeccable soul. I want you to know that just like the Hapy Eteru cannot remove the sacred Mdw Ntchr from the walls of Kemet or Kash, no matter how high the floodwaters, no one can pull you away from me. That is our destiny. Do not question it, my great Neb, but embrace it."

"I have embraced your soul ever since we met back in Napata. I have not mentioned it to you, but I thought of you often."

"Thank you, my divine Nswt, I needed that. You are the divine ruler from Waset not because of fate. I am your devoted wife not by chance but because our past lives and deeds and your present accomplishments have made it so. And I will be happiest when I'm by your side and by the side of Nswt Hemt Wrt Neferu and Mwt aa Iah and our loving son, Mentchu-hotep, my Neb."

* * *

The chief Medjay Jhutyms Ka-en-Heru came to visit me at the royal palace early one morning.

"Let's walk," he said. "How well do you know yourself, Shemsu Heru Mentchu-hotep?"

"Well, I think I'm on the correct path of self–knowledge, great Medjay." He continued, "Medjay spiritual traditions maintain that we do not know ourselves nearly as well as we think we do. When we were divine spiritual beings before we took on human form, we knew who we were and what our purpose was. But in our journey to earth, we became forgetful. Our task is to remember who we are once again and then stay in the path that leads to full self-awareness. I have watched you grow, first as a boy, now as a man. You have become Heru, but in becoming

Heru, we still have unfinished business in the northern delta."

I knew what he was saying was past due. Waset was strong, and Kash was strong. And we had built up our northernmost cities like Iwenet and Abedju. And it was my fourteenth year as Shemsu Heru Mentchu-hotep.

He spoke again after a long silence.

Each Kemet spiritual warrior must become Heru

Heru fights for liberation and freedom through excellence
When the human body temple is functioning with excellence
Mentally, physically, and spiritually

It turns against and eradicates diseased tissues

It destroys any element that would try to choke or disrupt its internal harmony

When we become Heru, we act with excellence

Mentally, we become Heru consciousness and Ma'at thinking
Physically, we develop strong, toned, conditioned sacred body temples

Spiritually, we are surrounded by love, and we become consciousness of our connection to the Ntchru

As Heru, we are in constant battle with the poisonous elements that are destroying Kemet culture and spirituality

We must oppose foreign domination and their worldview

Their eyes are like poison to Kemet

Kemet and Kash are one people, one mind, with one aim and one goal Excellence.

Because the time has come for the Kemetyu To reclaim our nation as guardians of Ma'at Like Heru, we must defend what we develop Until our last breath

Shemsu nu-n Heru Amen-Ra.

We stopped near the Hapy Eteru, and then he spoke again. "There is a revolt in Abedju amongst the Asiatics, and the northerners have attacked the sacred temple of Abedju, great Neb of Waset. We must crush this rebellion quickly."

"Is the northern leader Neb-Kau-Ra behind this?"

"*Tiw*, and they have built a great army with many warriors to defeat us." "Are we ready, Chief Medjay Jhutyms Ka-en-Heru?"

"We are, Shemsu Heru Mentchu-hotep" "Then we shall sail at sunrise tomorrow."

CHAPTER 10

WAR, THE UNITING OF A NATION-STATE

"Who are these Medjay? Are they just legend, or do they really exist? I want some answers. We are about to go into total war here, and I will not be embarrassed like my father was fourteen years ago. Where is my royal scribe? I need to send this chief of Waset a letter."

A strong warrior about six feet three and 230 pounds, chocolate complexion with a shiny bald head stood in the king's doorway.

"Who are you?"

"I am Commander Ta Ra from Sumeria, and I can tell you about your enemies from the south."

"Yes, Commander Ta Ra, I have seen you fight, and your reputation is well known among the warriors. Come in. They say you fight like three tigers rolled into one man. First who are these Medjay warriors? Are they real or just mythlogical phantoms of someone's embellished imagination?"

"I'm sorry to tell you this, my King, but they are very real and very dangerous. They have never been defeated in combat."

"Who have they beaten?" shouted the King.

"Your father for one." King Mery-Ka-Ra stood up straight in his chair. "They have fought throughout the known and unknown world, and all their enemies have lost. They come from the south near the source of the Hapy Eteru, deep into the interior of the unknown continent where no northerner has ever been. Their leaders seem to have some mystical powers of unknown energy."

"Stop right there. This is starting to sound like some children's fantasy story. How about the chief of Waset? What do you know about him?"

"He is a Medjay warrior also, Mentchu-Hotep, and he has surrounded himself with Medjay warriors."

"Is he really eight feet tall?"

"No, my King, he is a tall man, maybe six feet five and very powerful."

As the northern king stood up, with a very determined look on his face, he asked, "More powerful than me? The bottom line is, can we defeat them?"

* * *

Shemsu Heru Mentchu-hotep stood before his two royal wives, High Priestess Neferu and Priestess Tem.

"If I were a temple," he said with strong feelings, "you two would be my walls that allow me to reach great heights. My life is charged by you, my vision comes from you, and will continue to flow from you even when I'm gone. This I know. We are at war, and I need both of you to continue my work here while I am gone. Teach my son his responsiblities to the family, and keep him safe. I shall return as soon as I can. My mission now is victory and reorganization for our people."

Nswt Mwt Wrt Iah entered the room, and everyone stood up and bowed with respect.

"Mother, I'm so glad you could join us."

She walked up to her son and hugged him. "My son, when you defeat our northern enemies, you shall be a hero like Heru to our people. Your face shall grace the walls of great temples like Heru. Your face will be a face for our people to celebrate and remember like Shemsu Heru Narmer who united Upper and Lower Kemet. Heroes are not fantasized, they are real people. Heroes need to be celebrated and immortalized like the Ntchru. Without heroes and sheroes, a culture will never aspire to greatness. This is the message I bring you from the oricle of Amen-Ra. You will be victorious, my son. And I shall immortalize your name and your image, as well as your great works."

Hmt Nswt Wrt Neferu stood up as she spoke, "When you march out of Waset at sunrise, Shemsu Heru Mentchu-hotep, lead like you are the Nswt Bety who is a Medjay chief."

"What do you mean?"

"For the last fourteen years, you have shown your people your Ma'atian nature. That you are a gentle giant who is noble, good, and pure. But now you must show your ferocity. To lead lions, you must be a lion, to lead falcons, you must soar like a mighty falcon. Dress like a Medjay chief, but you will wear the *sekhmty* double crown because you are the royal ruler of Upper and Lower Kemet, the Nswt Bety, and the son of Ra. Priestess Tem made one specially for you."

Hmt Tem stood up and opened up a box and pulled out a magnificent red-and-white double crown, glittering with a golden cobra and vulture in front.

"It's breathtaking," he said.

That evening after everyone was asleep, Shemsu Heru Mentchu- hotep walked through the sacred temples of Iput Isut. All his training had come down to this, and he would rule one united nation-state, Sma Tawy, or die in the attempt. He knew he was not alone, and he could feel his great-grandfather walking beside him, as well as a host of other powerful ancestors whose names were lost but whose souls still lingered with him. He now knew what it meant to embrace the reality of your feelings that come to you from the world. In that moment, he began to use a different mode of cognition. And at that moment, he began to think with his heart.

The sky from the Sacred temple Iput Isut, Waset, the capital of Kemet

Mentchu-hotep sat down at the head of the great royal oval table with him on one end and the chief Medjay Jhutyms Ka-en-Heru at the other. To his right was the vizier Dagi; to the left, Hemt Nswt Wrt Neferu; next to her was Nswt Mwt Wrt Iah, the great royal mother of the Ntchru. The others around the table were his chancellor Medjay Khety-n-Ra, chief steward Medjay Bennu Henenu, Kashite Viscroy Medjay Ka-en-Jhutyms, head of security Medjay Akhtoy Ba-Heru, the Sdjawty treasurer Medjay Ipi, all the high priest and priestess, and a host of other important people that made Kemet function. The Shemsu Heru Mentchu-hotep stood up, and he could feel all eyes on him as he wore the Skhemty double crown. But this was not a time for speeches, it was a time for action.

"We all know why we are here—we are at war. Not only have they attacked Abedju, they have plundered our ancient burial grounds. So we are not only fighting for our nation but for our angry royal ancestors. Imagine with all your mind. Believe with all your heart that we will achieve victory with all our skills. Your thoughts constitute your prayers. Use thoughts and beliefs to create your realities wisely. Do not create thoughts that produce the illusion of limitation. Instead create thoughts that expand and extend for you that which you desire to expand and extend. Create thoughts that heal and unite you with the Divine Spirit. When we meet again like this, it will be a united two lands, Sema Tawy. I now introduce Chief Medjay Jhutyms Ka-en-Heru."

I sat as the chief Medjay spoke. My eyes peered the room. What strength and what beauty. This was our moment in time. I could feel it. We could feel it. As he looked up, he could see his great-grandfather smiling at him. Thousands of years from now, people will still remember our names because Kemet, the most powerful nation on earth, is about to move into our second great golden age.

* * *

"Scribe, tell the chief of Waset, Mentchu-hotep or whatever his name is, if he retreats from the city of Abedju, Khemenu, Zawty, and Meheze within two days by sunset, I will let him continue to rule the south. Also withdraw all your warriors from the eastern and western desert so we may renegotiate trade routes beween our two nations. If we do not receive a reply by the time stated, we will consider it an act of war, and you may lose everything you cherish and hold dear. King Mery-Ka-Ra. Make several copies so I know he will get it in time, now go."

"Ahh, Commander Ta Ra, did the king of Sumeria receive the gold?" "Yes, my lord, and you will have five thousand troops in two days." "Now what are my chances of winning?"

King Mery Ka-Ra was a big man, six feet four maybe three hundred pounds and a very skilled warrior. He towered over most of his opponents and usually beat them with just brute strength. He sat in council with his four commanders.

"In two days, we will attack. Our Sumerian troops will hit them at Khemenu and Zawty. Meanwhile, we will send ten thousand troops to Abedju and Iunet by midday. Our Sumerian troops should join us fresh and ready to destroy our enemies in Abedju. The next morning, we will finish them off by attacking Waset. Commanders, tell your warriors, as promised one half of all the gold, jewlery, and precious gifts are yours to keep. The gold and jewels we plundered at the royal cemetery in Abedju was nothing compared to what's waiting for us in Waset.

"This is going to be a very prosperous war, and the women you may take as many as you want, I know you love those black beauties from the south. But take no prisoners. Death to our enemies, slay them all. We will destroy their monuments and burn there temples and cities. I want the city of Waset charred with their worthless bodies and slashed-open flesh. When we are finished, I want flowing blood to be an example of my northern power. Remember, when we find their leaders, find me and bring them to me. I want to kill this Medjay Mentchu-hotep myself! Commander Ta Ra, I shall give you the honor of destroying this myth maker, Medjay Jhutyms. Then we will hang their bodies from our ships so everyone can see that the Medjay have been defeated. Poets shall write about our victory, and singers will sing songs about the defeat of the legendary Medjay. And my name will be Immortal King Mery Ka-Ra." Meanwhile, Chief Medjay Jhutyms Ka-en-Heru alongside Shemsu Heru Mentchu-hotep and the Medjay medju were sailing to the northern capital Herakleopolis with ten thousand Medjay warriors and five thousand Kemet warriors, a full day ahead of King Neb-Kau- Ra's plan. There was still five thousand Kemet and Medjay warriors in Abedju to protect their southern borders and five thousand Kemet and Medjay warriors still in the capital city of Waset as backup. You could feel the Kemet-Kash united force neatly molded into one unstoppable energy riding the Hapy Eteru.

"We know they have hired five thousand Sumerian warriors from the north, and they should arrive tomorrow by noon. I have already sent a message to my friend Ur-Nammu, the king of the Sumerians, apologizing for destroying his men. But this is not his war, and when sometimes you gamble foolishly, you lose. I have already given you the plans, and we shall be upon them in less than an hour. Clear your minds, and make your hearts pure and full of love, for this victory is for Ma'at. That's why we fight, and that is why we cannot lose. I can show you where the enemy is, but I cannot tell you what to see or what to do. That must come from the Creator Ntchru that resides inside you. Now listen to the Nswt Bety Sa Ra, Mentchu-hotep."

"I will be brief for you already know what to do and how to do it. We shall harm no women and children nor the elderly and sick. We shall not destroy properity or monuments, and we shall not violate any sacred temples. We are here to destroy our enemies. We are here to unite our two lands. The laws of civil war are different from the rules governing foreign wars because of ourstorical and historical relations and because of bonds of kinship and the common sacred sites throughout the country. Fight with Ma'at in your heart, Amen-Ra."

The ships were silent, and our warriors were ready.

* * *

"Mwt Aa Iah, where is Father?"

"He is completing his father, his grandfather, and his great-grandfather's great mission."

"He has left to fight the northerners. I must get my sword."
"Wait, young man, you're not going anywhere."

216

"No, you don't understand, Father said I could help him."
"I do understand, and you can but not fight."

"I have been training, Mwt aa."

"Your father needs your help when he comes back. Uniting the two lands and cleaning up the mess after a war takes much longer and much more organizational skills. Now go get your papyrus scrolls."

"Are you making this up, Mwt Aa Iah?"

"Now why would I do that to the crown prince Mentchu-hotep?"

* * *

As we approached their headquarters, several of our ships docked and maybe two thousand troops entered by land a mile away. We continued straight ahead in the silence of the soft morning light. The Medjay warriors were much different from most warriors because you could not really see them. Despite their multitudes, they remained all but invisible. The Medjay and Kemetic troops just blended into the landscape when needed that would soon fill the air with thunder.

As we approached their empty warships, part of our fleet sailed passed them. They were alarmed and sent out a war signal, but it was already too late. Our Kashite bowmen sent fire arrows onto their ships by the hundreds, and within minutes, their ships were in flames. Three thousand troops confronted them at the shore. We sailed on into the capital and to their royal palace where they had maybe three thousand troops assembled. I looked over at the chief Medjay Jhutyms Ka-en-Heru, and he had a smile on his face. We outnumbered them here two to one. Some of our warriors docked, and several ships sailed past them. We would attack from three fronts.

Back at their mililtary camp by the time their warships had sank and completely burned up, they were defeated. Our warriors had ascended upon their military camp from every possible angle—from the shore, from behind, and from both sides. They didn't know which way to turn between the fire arrows burning their campsite like a barn fire to skilled swordsmen, spears, and arrows coming at them from every direction. They had more soldiers, but it was of little to no significance. They were outsmarted and definitely outskilled and, in the confusion, just got in each other's way.

"Come, my king, there is a canal that leads back to the Hapy Eteru, and we can escape to Het-ka-Ptah and regroup and join our Sumerian warriors."

"What about our ten thousand troops?"

"We have already lost, my king, if we can see them at our front gates. That means they have routed our troops at the military base. Look, my king, do you see the smoke? Our fleet has been destroyed, and their strength has not even been tested yet.

"And our three thousand troops out front?" shouted the king. "They are already dead, my king. We are wasting time."

* * *

We could not believe our eyes. The northern troops were lined up at the shore like sitting ducks. Even with their shields, our Kashite bowmen cut them down by the hundreds with their arrows. Our Medjay warriors leaped out of the ships and attacked straight on while our Kemet warriors attacked the two sides. The Mejay medju headed straight for the royal palace. We slashed our way through their troops like cutting through wheat. All around us, you could hear battle cries and screams and unanswered prayers. The Medjay and Kemet warriors looked unstoppable. Once the Medjay Medju was inside the palace, we were challenged by maybe fifty northern warriors to our eleven Medjay. The fighting was fierce, and at close range, we were a fearsome sight.

I saw Chief Medjay Jhutyms ram his spear through two warriors at one time. Heads were flying, and I saw Medjay Akhtoy Ba-Heru kick a warrior's teeth out of his mouth, then plunge his sword through his midsection. I killed at least three or four northerners myself, and they never knew they were dead before they started. I was impressed that they fought to the last man. When we searched the rooms, we found only women and children. Medjay Ka-en-Jhutyms found a gardener hiding in the flowers out back and made him talk. He explained the king, his three wives, and about ten warriors escaped by way of a canal that rejoins Hapy Eteru about a mile downstream.

* * *

"What can you see, Hemet Nswt Wrt Neferu?" asked Hmt Nswt Tem. They all held hands around a large table with a crystal Mr Khut (pyramid) in the center of the table.

"We are victorious, but the war is not over yet."

"What do you mean, Mother? Explain," said the crown prince Mentchu-hotep.

"Their king has escaped, and he is heading to Het-Ka-Ptah with his three wives and a small group of northern warriors."

"They are like scared dogs on the run, and Father will catch them." "Wait, I see a large force of foreign warriors moving toward the northern king. Their leader is wearing red."

* * *

Shemsu Heru Sa Ra Mentchu-hotep whispered to his chief Medjay commander Jhutyms Ka-en-Heru, and then he spoke to Commander Medjay Ka-en-Jhutyms, "Send the messenger birds to Abedju to send four thousand troops to Het-Ka Ptah. We will end this war by tomorrow before Ra sets in the horizon."

Our Medjay and Kemet warriors suffered very few casualties. They fought like a well-trained polished veteran machine. Now they would heal our wounded and carry our dead and place them on ships to be buried at home. Spirits were high because we had crushed our foes like a mighty storm, but we knew the real fight was yet to come. And we were ready.

* * *

"May I speak with the vizier Dagi please? Tell him it is Shemsu Heru Tut-ankh-Ra from Napata. I have come to help and anyway I can."

"Thank you, great Neb, but please wait here. I shall return shortly," said the Medjay warrior guard at the front gate of the temple of Iput Isut.

"Vizier Dagi," as the Mejay knelt on one knee, "there is a man at our front gate with several Napata warriors who says he is Shemsu Heru Tut-Ankh-Ra from Napata."

"*Tiw*, I will come with you. Take me to him." Excitement ran through Vizier Dagi's mind because he was a young student of Shemsu Heru Tut-ankh-Ra when he studied in Napata as

220

a youth. *What an honor,* he thought. He told another royal guard to fetch Hemet Nswt Tem and her son, the crown prince Mentchu-hotep, and to meet them in the royal courtyard.

Vizier Dagi could not believe it with his own eyes. The Shemsu Heru Tut-Ankh Ra had hardly aged at all. He knew he had to be twice his age, but they looked like peers. Vizier Dagi knelt on one knee and placed his palms together with great respect, and his guards did the same.

"Dua Ntchr, Ntchru great Neb, Shemsu Heru Tut-Ankh-Ra en Napata."

He smiled as he dismounted his beautiful black horse, returning their greetings of respect.

"*Dua ye m hotep,* Vizier Dagi. I am pleased to see you again. It has been many years, and I see you have done well." They hugged in brothership.

"But I come with seven thousand Napata warriors and one hundred elephants. They await your command at the sixth cataract, the border between Kemet and Kash outside of the city of Abu. I also have an urgent message from Ur-Nammu of the newly reorganized Sumerian kingdom, and he says he has sent no troops to fight against Kemet or his Medjay brothers. These are wild Asiatics called the Gutins and Kassites from the Zargos Mountains who have been causing much turmoil and confusion in Asia. He himself has fought and chased them out of Sumeria.

"Father, is that you?"

"*Tiw,* my royal daugther Tem," as she ran into his arms. "And this is your son?"

"Tiw," she said.

"He has grown since I last saw him. He will be tall like his father.

Where is my other daughter, Hemet Nswt Neferu?"

"She is at the sacred temple of Het Heru, praying for our Nswt Mentchu-hotep's victory."

"Why are you here, Father?"

"To lend suport to our family. Can you find Hem Tepy Kha-f-Ptah for me, my daughter? I must speak to him."

"Mother, he is on the west bank, working," said the crown prince Mentchu-hotep.

"Great Vizier Dagi, it is extremely important that I speak to Hem Tepy Kha-f-Ptah."

"I will have several of my royal guards take you to him," replied Vizier Dagi.

When Shemsu Heru Sa Ra Mentchu-hotep and his fleet of warriors reached Het-Ka-Ptah, he was greeted only by a few priest from the temple. The Medjay medju along with the chief Medjay Jhutyms Ka- en-Heru greeted the Hem Sem Tepy of Het-Ka-Ptah.

"*Dua Ptah, Anedg hr ek Ptah* [homage to thee, Ptah]. How may I serve you?" said the head priest.

Shemsu Heru Mentchu-hotep spoke, "Dua Ptah, Anedg hr ek Ptah. We come to restore Ma'at and to reunite our two great lands into one nation. Your king, Mery-Ka-Ra, who represents esfet is on the run. We have defeated his forces at their Herakleopolitan seat of government, and he has hired foreign troops to fight for him. We have come in the name of Mentchu Heru who fights for Amen-Ra to destroy him and return Ma'at to our two lands."

All the priests from the temple of Het-Ka-Ptah knelt on both knees and gave praise to Ptah. We, the Medjay, also knelt on one knee to return their respect and praise.

Once they all rose, there Hem Sem Tepy spoke, "The king's wives are here in the Holy of Holies with several bodyguards, but the king has fled to greet his arriving troops from the north."

"Dua Ntchr, thank you. You may return to your priestly duties. We will take charge from here. No harm will come to your priest and priestess, the king's wives, your sacred temples, or any of the village people." Shemsu Heru Sa Ra Mentchu-hotep turned and looked over at the chief Medjay Jhutyms Ka-en-Heru and said, "You know what to do."

The chief Medjay waved his sacred spear, and the Kemet fleet quickly moved into fighting positions. And as the various commanders took charge of their warriors, the mind of Shemsu Heru Sa Ra Mentchu- hotep was already in full battle mode. He wanted to rule Upper and Lower Kemet even when he was in his mother's womb. This desire burned in his consciousness even before he had a body. It was his great- grandfather's desire. And now the only thing in the way was King Mery Ka-Ra and his Sumerian mercenaries. He longed to feel King Mery Ka-Ra's blood on his sword due to his greed, his unspiritual lifestyle, and his disrespect of their ancestors and sacred shrines and monuments. He had to die by his sword, not the tip of his arrow. Somehow that was not personal enough. He wanted to look into his eyes, a man he'd never met, but who denied him the missing piece of total unity, the red crown—Desrt.

My enemy is a disease, and it has a particular identity like a virus. It is an intelligent entity in its own right. It has its own desires, force of energy, and reality. It too is a self-organized system that wants to destroy me. And I will not stop until I have eliminated it from my consciousness and from the soil of Kemet. To kill King Mery Ka-Ra would be to fill himself, his great- grandfather, his sons, and to complete his father's incomplete mission. He would not only be filled, but also all their souls would be filled with power and peace that he and they had never known. He did not hate King Mery-ka-Ra, but reciprocity could only come from his destruction. Only then could Ma'at be restored.

* * *

"There, over there are our Sumerian warriors," The king shouted out. He had been really uptight the whole trip. Just the thought of losing his kingdom without even swinging his sword was unthinkable in his mind, and his internal anger just grew.

"Where is your commander in chief?" the king yelled. Someone yelled back at their boat. Commander Ta Ra translated that for the king and then maneuvered their small vessel into position so that the king could mount their vessel.

"Grab this rope!" a Sumerian warrior yelled out. The king's boat was pulled alongside their vessel, and a ladder was dropped for them to enter. The Sumerian commander was easy to spot as he was a huge man, maybe six feet six tall and about three hundred pounds with a light brown complexion, with a tightly curled beard and hair, dressed in all red. But the majority of his warriors were not Sumerian at all.

"Where are your warriors?" said there chief. In a Sumerian tongue, Commander Ta Ra spoke for the king.

"The Medjay destroyed his entire military." "Are you serious?" said the commander. "Yes, I am very serious, my lord."

The king grabbed Ta Ra by the arm. "What did he say?"

"He wants to know what is your plan."

$$* * *$$

Commander Akhtoy yelled out, "Coming ten degrees southwest, several enemy vessels approach. They are waving white flags. They seem to be Ta-Sety bowmen vessels."

"Let them in," said Shemsu Heru Nswt Bety Mentch-hotep. "What could they possibly want?" said Chief Medjay Jhutyms Ka-en-Heru, knowing that they were responsible for killing the Shemsu Heru Intef with a poison arrow.

"Let Ka-en-Jhutyms handle this, my chief commander."

He nodded his head with approval. The Ta-Sety bowmen were warned to stay in their vessels. Our warship sailed to meet them. The chief of the Ta-Sety bowmen with his son asked to come aboard. We offered them water and chairs, but the chief of the Ta-Sety bowmen with his son fell on their hands and knees.

"Please accept these three sacred bows as a token of our frienship. We know we have foolishly fought against you in the past and even challenged you even when you came in peace. Medjay Ka-en-Jhutyms, we owe you our lives, and we are willing to die for you and Shemsu Heru Mentchu-hotep of Kemet!"

"What do you propose?" said Ka-en-Jhutyms.

"Let us, the Ta-Sety bowmen, lead your attack against these foreign invaders. We know their general and their tactics. We have fought with them and against them, and we know how to defeat them. Our three thousand warriors are about equal to their six thousand troops."

"I thought they had five thousand troops?"

"More than one thousand Lybians and Amorites from the Delta have joined them. They have much to gain if the Gutians and Kassites are victorious. You know we have our spies." The chief bowmen looked at Chief Medjay Jhutyms and myself and said, "We know your Medjay can do what we do and even better, but please let us show our gratitude. Please allow us to pay our dept as warriors and as brothers. If there is no reciprosity, Ma'at cannot come into existence. We know that my son's arrow pierced your father's body. We cannot bring your father back, but we can help you unite your nation. Give us thirty mintues before your attack. Please, that is all we ask for."

Chief Medjay Jhutyms Ka-en-Heru walked up to the chief bowmen and said, "If this is a trick, I promise you there will be no Ta-Sety bowmen left on earth. You and your people will be a distant memory floating in the wind of eternity."

The chief said, "I know. I know now you are the greatest warriors on earth and heaven," as he bowed his head to exit.

"Shadow the Ta-Sety ships. We cannot take any chances. Everything else is as planned. They, the Ta-Sety bowmen, will scatter these foreign invaders, and we will clean them up on land and water. My Medjay medju, these are the same warriors you faced in the eastern desert. These wild Asians are strong, but their swordsmen's skills are only fair. And they also use a battle ax, very deadly, and they are fierce and will fight like they welcome death. They fight like rabid dogs, never full of enough blood. And the raping of your daughters possess them, and the annallation of your sons ignite them. They are soulless and vengeful. So you must not show any mercy because they will fight to their very last breath."

* * *

"Hem Tepy Kha-f-Ptah, it is so good to see you. We miss you in Napata." He bowed his head first and gave a Napata hand salute, then they embraced, and he returned the smile.

"But that is not why you are here, my father's brother, Shemsu Heru Tut–ankh-Ra."

"Can you warn your grandfather that he is not fighting Sumerians but Asiatic invaders from the Zargos Mountains called Gutians, Kossites, and Amorites."

Kha-f-Ptah closed his eyes as he sat motionless. Shemsu Heru Tut- Ankh-Ra, the ruler of one of the strongest countries in Afraka, watched his gifted brother's son as he stood in silence for about five minutes.

"My grandfather knows, and he is in no danger. Victory is all but sealed."

"Your father—"

"I know. He is the new viceroy of Sumeria. I have already expressed my joy for him."

"You knew I was here."

"I felt your presence over the last day as you entered my force field." "My daughter Tem does not know?"

"No, but your eldest son Medjay Ipi knows. He has grown strong with the Medjay force."

"My eldest son, Medjay Ipi, I miss him so much. He has always been so strong. He will not come home and rule after me, will he?"

"No, not in Napata. Your second son, Prince Piye, will rule after your long reign, my Neb. Medjay Ipi will eventually become the vizier for the Nswt Bety Mentchu-hotep and his son. And because the son will not be a strong leader, it is important that Vizier Ipi remain as a strong leader here in Kemet."

"I see. Watch over them for me, my brother's son."

"That is why I am here. I will do my best, my father's brother," he said as their heads bowed.

"One more thing—"

"I know, my mother's sister is here. She is a Djedi along with my grandfather's second Medjay wife. Their force is strong and powerful."

* * *

The clash of steel against steel rang out as did the shouts of warriors— warriors falling, clutching at mortal wounds and screaming for aid that did not arrive. The Medjay and Kemet forces were at their very best because the Asiactics were fighting their fight. The Ta-Sety bowmen had routed and burned their ships, causing them to flee and run for cover as they blackened the sky with arrows. Many of the Asiactics ran recklessly into our swords and spears, and blood and body parts covered the earth for miles.

"Where is their king?" I shouted to the chief Medjay Jhutyms Ka-en-Heru.

"He is in the eye of the storm. Follow me." The chief Medjay Jhutyms Ka-en-Heru pulled out his two swords from his back sword case and began fighting his way toward the center. He ran and fought like the Ntchru as his two swords cut through the Asiatic warriors like hot butter with the Medjay medju right behind him. He just plowed into and over his enemies almost effortlessly, leaving a trail of dead bodies straight to the center of the war.

"There they are," spoke the chief Medjay Jhutyms Ka-en-Heru. "I want the big one," said Ka-en-Jhutyms.

"The king is mine," I yelled out.

Medjay Ipi said, "I'll take the Sumerian trader."

The rest of the Medjay medju surrounded them so that there would be no interference.

Up until this point, it was a one-sided affair. The foreigners were completly surrounded. As they ran from the arrows of the Ta-Sety bowmen and their flaming ships, they ran into the death traps of Medjay and Kemetic swords and spears. They were chopped down like fields of wheat or barley. Blood, limbs, and cries filled the air.

Directly in the center of all the action was the beginning of the final battle. The huge Sumerian chief swung his large sword at Medjay Ka-en-Jhutyms, knocking him back at first, putting a smile to his face. *Aah, this is going to be good,* he thought. He returned the attack with two, three—no, four quick strikes to the Sumerian's head and then a straight launch to his midsection, but the skillful Sumerian general blocked the strikes and sidestepped the lunge, almost falling off-balance. The Sumerian tried to retaliate with his sword, but Ka-en Jhutyms was one step ahead of him, blocking his sword attack with his own sword and then throwing a reverse wheel kick to the Sumerian's head. Blood squirted from his mouth as he began to swing wildly with his sword, but the Medjay kept the pressure on, stepping close inside, shield against shield, sword against sword, then reversing his attack, spinning with his sword and cutting the huge Sumerian general across his shoulder and backside. The Sumerian general grunted and smiled at the Medjay.

"You will have to do better than that if you want to live Medjay!" shouted the Sumerian general.

They circled each other for a few seconds, then the Sumerian general kicked dirt up into Medjay Ka-en-Jhutyms's face and lunged with his sword at the Medjay's heart at the same time. Blindly, Medjay Ka-en- Jhutyms blocked with his shield using the eyes of Set, sidestepped and countered the attack at the same moment, stripping the sword from the huge Sumerian's hand and then cutting him across his chest as the Sumerian general retreated. The general tasted the blood from his chest with his hand and smiled, pulling out his whip quickly from his belt. He tried to capture the Medjay's leg, but again Ka-en-Jhutyms prejudged his move, stepping in close out of range of the whip and striking two quick kicks toward the Sumerian's head, pushing him back off balance. Then with a quick Medjay special sword technique, he cut the whip almost completely out of his hand. And before the Sumerian could recover, he spun quickly with a low attack, cutting the Sumerian general across his large calf muscle, causing him to fall to one knee. Medjay Ka-en-Jhutyms then leaped into air, over the Sumerian's shield, and kicked him square in the nose, sending the huge Sumerian general tumbling backward to the ground with blood pouring from his face. The Sumerian general wiped the blood from his eyes and face and pulled out his battle ax.

The northern king Mery Ka-Ra and Shemsu Heru Mentchu-hotep locked eyes as they circled each other, looking for any human weakness.

King Mery Ka-Ra felt that if he could kill this Medjay king Mentchu- hotep, he could possibly change the course of the battle and still win, regaining his throne and his land. Shemsu Heru Mentchu-hotep on the other hand saw this totally different. He had been training for this battle his whole life. He had killed his northern opponent at least one thousand times in his dreams. He had practiced killing the king with all five of his mastered weapons plus his bare hands in countless ways. At this moment, it was just a matter of how King Mery Ka-Ra was going to die, not if he was going to die.

Shemsu Heru Mentchu-hotep had summoned all the powerful Ntchru in his consciousness to be with him at this moment. He was no longer Mentchu-hotep, the ruler of Waset, but he had transformed into Heru, Shango, Setsh, Mentchu, Neith, Skhmet, Memmon, Nemrod, Annu Aa, Sobek, the black panther, and Heru Bes all rolled into one. He would fight like the Ntchru, and victory would not be denied.

Medjay Ipi looked at his Sumerian opponent. They stood about the same height, weight, and even the same color of chocolate brown.

"You are the Sumerian trader called Ta Ra." He paused as they stared at each other. "My people saved your life, trained you, raised you, educated you. And your reward is their betrayal for a few pieces of gold? You shall pay not only with your life, but I will destroy your soul. I will cut your head off and pull your heart out and burn them both on my altar with a special spell sending nightmares into the minds of all traders who pass Kemet's borders like you!"

"You talk well, Medjay warrior from Napata, and you seem to know things you shouldn't know. But now let's see if your sword skills can match up to all the hype behind the Medjay legends."

"If it is my sword skills you want to see, I will prolong your life and lengthen our battle so before you die, you will not be disappointed in my sword skills." Ta Ra grew angry and lashed out with his sword attack, swinging sideways hard against the shield of Medjay Ipi who blocked his attack effortlessly.

"Anger will cloud your mind and only lead you to a quick death." Medjay Ipi then quickly swung overhead with his sword, then to the side, and with blinding speed, spun in the opposite direction, cutting the commander Ta Ra across his face. Ta Ra smiled as he admired the Medjay's skills. But he had a few tricks of his own, he thought. His attacks were relentless, but the Medjay Ipi countered every move. Medjay Ipi then decided to give Ta Ra a sword lesson, swinging his sword circular. When steel touched steel, he dropped low, reversing the blade that cut Ta Ra across his right thigh. Then he jumped over his shield, kicking Ta Ra to the side of his head. Ta Ra stumbled backward and came back swinging his sword. Medjay Ipi did the same move in the opposite direction, cutting his left thigh.

Ta Ra tried to do his own spinning tecnique, but Medjay Ipi countered in the opposite direction and sent his sword through Ta Ra's left arm, making it difficult for the Sumerian to hold his own shield. Then kicking and striking the shield with great power to the left, Medjay Ipi knocked the shield out of Ta Ra's hand and quickly spun back to the right and cut Ta Ra's left arm completely off. Ta Ra did not go into shock or show any extreme signs of pain, but like a well-trained warrior, he rebounded quickly with an strong offense attack of his own. Medjay Ipi threw down his shield and fought Ta Ra with one arm behind his back, blocking his attack with his sword. Then while looking into Ta Ra's eyes, Medjay Ipi, with blinding Medjay speed, thrust his sword through Ta Ra's stomach and back out. Ta Ra fell to his knees, and just as quick, the Medjay stepped inside with a knee to his face, then cutting off his sword arm. Ta Ra still on his knees, armless, looked over toward the king Mery Ka-Ra. And the king jumped back as blood squirted into his face and Ta Ra's head rolled at his feet.

Many of the foreign warriors were distracted by the terrible defeat of Comander Ta Ra as Medjay Ipi stood in front of his headless and armless body with his heart in one hand and his bloody sword in the other. This only made the Medjay and Kemetic warriors fight harder. If the Asiactics could run, they would have, but there was nowhere to go—arrows were still cutting them down from behind by the Ta-Sety bowmen while heads and arms were flying like a human storm. Screams and cries filled the air partially muffled by warriors chants.

Three-fourths of the foreigners were already dead, and the earth and Hapy was covered red and filled with the foreigners' blood.

The king Mery Ka-Ra kicked Ta Ra's head to the side and wiped Ta Ra's blood from his own face. He thought how sharp the Medjay's sword had to be to severe his head in a single stroke. The Sumerian chief also pushed Ta Ra's head to the side with his foot as he held his large shield in his battered left hand, now ready to do battle with his specially designed battle ax.

Medjay Ka-en-Jhutyms gave his opponent a moment to regroup before completing his mission. He placed his sword back into its holster case strapped across his back. The Medjay Ka-en-Jhutyms pulled out a gold and silver dagger from his waist that was given to him by his father when he became a Medjay commander in his father's elite warrior forces. He smiled at his already beaten opponent, the Sumerian chief. He quickly stepped in close, faking low and striking high, cutting the Sumerian across his forehead. The Sumerian chief tried to block with his heavy shield, but it was too late. The Medjay blocked the inside of the shield with his bare hand, stripping the large shield from his grip and lifting his huge body into the air and throwing him over his shoulder. The Sumerian chief landed with a loud thump that shook the earth. The Sumerian chief struggled to his feet only to meet a crushing kick to his face that sent him back kissing the earth face-first this time. The Sumerian chief rolled away from his opponent with only his battle ax in his right hand with blood and dirt covering his face. He could now feel the pain in the fingers on his left hand, and they were all broken from the Medjay's throwing attack. He tried to swing his battle ax at the Medjay, but Ka-en-Jhutyms kicked him in his throat so fast he did not see the move. He only felt the pain, and before he could strike again, his battle ax was stripped from his right hand, and with a continuing circular movement, his throat was cut as he sank to his knees. Medjay Ka-en-Jhutyms wiped the blood from his dagger, returning it to its case. He turned while spinning in a circular motion toward the Sumerian chief, pulling his sword out all in the same motion and cutting the Sumerian chief's head completely off in a continuous move. Again the blood squirted into the face of the king Mery Ka Ra.

For a moment, the king Mery Ka-Ra could not see as he wiped the blood from his red face covered in blood from his two Sumerian commanders.

The legend of the Medjay is true, he thought. Every strike he had made was blocked effortlessly by Shemsu Heru Mentchu-hotep, and the king was cut already five or six times on his face, arms, and legs. It was like the Medjay king was possessed, and at certain times, he even looked like a black panther.

"Weren't you told we were the greatest warriors on earth and heaven?" said Shemsu Heru Mentchu-hotep as he kicked the king in his stomach, forcing him to step back again.

The king swung his sword with all his might at his Medjay opponent. Shemsu Heru blocked his sword with his shield and leaped into the air, thrusting his sword past the king's shield and into the king's shoulder. Then with two mighty blows with his sword and a lunging side kick, he knocked the three-hundred-pound king off his feet. Shemsu Heru twirled in the air with a mighty whirling kick landing on the king's head, which seemed to daze the king. The king tried to block with his shield, but with his blurry vision, it looked like the Medjay had turned into a huge black panther. The king tried to block the panther's attack with his shield, and the mighty black panther ripped his shield, holding his left arm completely out of its socket with multiple clawing techniques. Then the Medjay Shemsu Heru Mentchu-hotep thrusted his sword into the midsetion of the king through all his armor. The king Mery Ka Ra looked at the blood gushing from his missing left arm and midsection in disbelief. Holding tightly to his sword, he swung with all his remaining strength. The Medjay kicked the sword from his hand and countered his attack by cutting his remaining arm off. Then he leaped, swirling into the air maybe nine feet with his sword severing the king's head in a single stroke. Now all three heads of the enemies stood side by side in the dirt. Lightning struck the earth next to the fallen body of the king. The fighting stopped everywhere, and all the Asiatics dropped their weapons and fell to their knees. They had never come against such fierce warriors in all their history as warriors. There was a dead silence in the air. And then a loud thunder echoed behind more lightning, with a white smoke surrounding the body of the dead king and Mentchu-hotep.

Everyone saw the huge black panther vanish into the smoke and transform into Mentchu-hotep, as he stood up with the bloody sword in his right hand and the king's heart in his left, blood dripping from his mouth. No one said a word.

The chief Medjay Jhutyms Ka-en-Heru walked over and hugged Mentchu-hotep. Then he whispered in his ear, "Your great-grandfather is gone, reciprocity is done. They are all in Ma'at."

* * *

The whole Medjay medju surrounded me. We placed the three heads and two hearts together in one pile as we all hugged as one. The rain began to fall, and we knew that was a cleansing sign from the heavens and that Nut and Tefnut, along with the Ntchru Mentchu and Heru, were satisfied.

The Medjay medju stayed embraced for a long time. Then as quickly as the rain came, it was gone. Ra emerged, and a rainbow filled the sky. The fighting was done, and the battle cries faded away. Now a deep silence fell over the land, covering everything left alive like a thick blanket. But after a fleeting moment, the cries of the wounded tore the silence into fragments that remained, if at all, only in memory. There were the calls for water, calls for help that could never come, and sometimes a simple prayer for death. Into the living, surviving warriors, the cries traveled, and they lodged in the deep recesses of their minds and would not let go. We would hear them for as long as we live.

The chief Medjay Jhutyms Ka-en-Heru gave the orders to secure the prisoners and start cleanup. After a long silence, I spoke, "Bring forth the messenger birds. Summon the scribes, for they must record and tell our story just as the Ntchru witnessed our victory. We must restore Ma'at, drive the foreigners from the delta and completely off our land. Ta Mry, our beloved land, is united again. Tell our wives and children and all our beloved family of Waset that we will return to Waset in one month from tomorrow. Amen-Ra, through the might and power of Mentchu, is victorious."

I knelt at the feet of Chief Medjay Jhutyms Ka-en-Heru, and so did all the Medjay medju. The chief Medjay placed his hand on my shoulder as he spoke, "It will be 250 years before they return with military might. We still have much work to do. We all looked up into the sky and saw a meteorite falling from the sky with a long fire tail that then broke up into several pieces. That was a sign for us of a job well-done but not complete.

End of Book One

ABOUT THE AUTHOR

Mfundishi Jhutyms Ka n Heru Hassan Kamau Salim is a holistic Kultural custodian of traditional Afrikan Kulture and ancient Kemet.

Mfundishi (pronounced M-foon-dee-shee) Is an Author, poet, playwright, Story-Teller, Professor of Afrikan Studies, Kemetologists, Kemet High Priest, Spiritual Guide, lecturer, motivational speaker and Grand master in the Mentchu Afrikan combat system of Kupigana Ngumi.

He is a teacher and professor of Afrikan studies who specializes in the Nile Valley Kulture of North east Afrika and the Mdw Ntchr (Hieroglyphics), and has taught nationally in the United States of America, the Caribbean's, Europe and Africa, lecturing in over 150 Collages and Universities. He has traveled to over 25 Afrikan countries and has visited the Nile Valley over 27 times. He was initiated as a High Priest and a Chief in Africa, later to become a Kemet High Priest of Kera Jhuty Heru Neb Hu Per Ankh (House of Life), a 501 (c) 4 non-profit spiritual, educational and Kultural organization. He is one of the rare certified Afrikan-centered teachers of the Mdw Netcher (Egyptian Hieroglyphics) and a Doctor of Naturopathy. For over 50 years, he trained in the Mentchu holistic healing sciences and is a Grand Master in the Afrikan Mentchu Warrior science of Kupigana Ngumi Aha Kemet and the Kemet meditation and breathing system of Ma'at Akhw Ba

Ankh. He also holds an 8th degree Black belt in Shaolin Hung Gar Kung-Fu. He is the author of several books. Kupigana Ngumi, his book, "Spiritual Warriors Are Healers", is a best seller among Afrikan bookstores nationwide and his new book released in 216 "Menchu- hotep and the Spirit of the Medjay".

Today Mfundishi operate a Kultural holistic vending both in Harlem, New York called, "Black Gold, 125th Street and Malcolm X Blvd and a Harlem base Kemety Spiritual Shrine, that offers a wide range of programs, services and products – from individual consulting, to seminars, retreats, rites of passages, cultural trips, conferences and keynote speeches. To contact Mfundishi, please visit their websites www.mfundishijhutyms.org. or Facebook: Mfundishi Jhutyms, Email: mfundishijhutyms@gmail.com

www.ingramcontent.com/pod-product-compliance
Lightning Source LLC
Chambersburg PA
CBHW060911120626
46553CB00001B/280